Helping Young Children
Develop Social Skills

Brooks/Cole Professional Books

Consulting Editor: C. Eugene Walker

Family Therapy and Beyond: A Multisystemic Approach to Treating the Behavior Problems of Children and Adolescents
Scott W. Henggeler and Charles M. Borduin

Changing Expectations: A Key to Effective Psychotherapy
Irving Kirsch

Panic Disorders and Agoraphobia: A Comprehensive Guide for the Practitioner
John R. Walker, G. Ron Norton, and Colin A. Ross, Editors

The History of Clinical Psychology in Autobiography, Volumes I and II
C. Eugene Walker, Editor

Helping Young Children Develop Social Skills: The Social Growth Program
Cheryl A. King and Daniel S. Kirschenbaum

HELPING YOUNG CHILDREN DEVELOP SOCIAL SKILLS:
The Social Growth Program

CHERYL A. KING
University of Michigan

DANIEL S. KIRSCHENBAUM
Northwestern University

Brooks/Cole Publishing Company
Pacific Grove, California

A CLAIREMONT BOOK

Consulting Editor: C. Eugene Walker

Brooks/Cole Publishing Company
A Division of Wadsworth, Inc.

Printed in the United States of America

10 9 8 7 6 5 4 3 2 1

Library of Congress Cataloging in Publication Data

King, Cheryl A. Polewach, [date]
    Helping young children develop social skills : the social growth
program / Cheryl A. King, Daniel S. Kirschenbaum.
        p.   cm. — (Brooks/Cole professional books)
    Includes bibliographical references and index.
    ISBN 0-534-17016-1
    1. Socialization.   2. Social skills in children—Study and
teaching—United States.   I. Kirschenbaum, Daniel S., [date]
HQ783.K58   1992
362.2'083—dc20   91-27757
                                                    CIP

Sponsoring Editor: Claire Verduin
Editorial Assistant: Gay C. Bond
Manufacturing Buyer: Vena M. Dyer
Production Editor: Joan Marsh
Production Assistant: Merrill Peterson
Manuscript Editor: Victoria Nelson
Permissions Editor: Carline Haga
Interior Design: Cynthia Bogue
Cover Design: Vernon T. Boes
Interior Illustration: Duane Bibby
Typesetting: Kachina Typesetting
Printing and Binding: R. R. Donnelley & Sons

To our children
Janna and Michelle (C.A.K.)
Alexander and Maxwell (D.S.K.)

PREFACE

This book is designed for mental health professionals (guidance counselors, psychologists, social workers, psychiatrists), students in training, and paraprofessionals who are involved in helping young children (5 to 9 years) relate to others in socially adaptive ways. Our intent is to provide a complete handbook that will assist the school-based or community-based practitioner in developing and implementing a sensitive, effective intervention program for a child or group of children with social and emotional adjustment problems.

Social skills training has become a dominant method of intervention for many professionals who work in schools, clinics, and private practice offices. Large-scale community and school-based intervention programs have also trained paraprofessionals to work with children on social skills in an effort to expand and extend the delivery of helping resources. Despite this accelerated interest in social skills, there are surprisingly few handbooks oriented toward promoting social skills in young elementary school children. Perhaps of greater importance, existing handbooks often present skills training as an automated process without taking into account children's developmental levels, each child's individual characteristics, and the potentially powerful impact of the practitioner-child relationship.

The book begins with three chapters that provide a conceptual and empirical basis for the Social Growth Program, an outgrowth of our own program experiences over the last sixteen years as well as the past work of many others in this field. Chapter 1 describes the nature and importance of social adjustment among young elementary school children. Chapter 2 discusses three perspectives on young children's social adjustment—social learning, developmental, and individual differences—along with an illustrative case example. Chapter 3 presents an overview of major, forerunner early intervention efforts and their empirical basis. Chapter 4 describes the Social Growth Program's goals and rationale and provides procedural information on designing and implementating an intervention program with an individual child or groups of children. Chapter 5 presents information on screening children for large-scale programs and on the assessment of children's social adjustment. This chapter also describes how to develop individualized social growth goals for each participating child. Chapter 6 is an extended chapter that presents the nine social skills modules. Each module is presented with goals, a rationale, and detailed preparation ideas in addition to information on how to conduct an individual or group session. Finally, FOR ME homework assignments and FOR MY PARENTS (AND TEACHERS) take-home papers are included to help children generalize their improved social skills to other settings.

We would like to thank many people for their part in making this book possible. Much of our program development work was made possible by a grant from the office of Human Development Services, Department of Health and Human Services to the State of Wisconsin (Dan Kirschenbaum and Mary Conroy, Principal Investigators). We thank the staff of the Wisconsin Office of Mental Health for their assistance in implementing the Wisconsin Early Intervention Program, especially Dan Crossman, Susan Staab, and Susan Davis. We also want to thank the group leaders (Dorothy Barber, Lorraine Breininger, Bobbie Haig, Mary Richardson, Win Severson, and Eva Wolf) for their enthusiasm, dedication, and creative energy, which resulted in many suggestions that have been incorporated into the Social Growth Program modules. The patience and helpfulness of the Wisconsin Heights School District staff is also gratefully acknowledged. In a similar manner, we owe many thanks to those staff members and schools involved in Cincinnati's Social Skills Development Program.

A special thanks goes to Claire Verduin for her helpful stance and steady encouragment, to Eugene Walker for his valuable suggestions concerning the scope of this book, and to Victoria Nelson for her careful and thoughtful copy editing. Jeff Dobek is also sincerely thanked for his good-natured and skillful help in typing the original draft of this book. Finally, we would like to express our personal thanks to several important and special persons. Cheryl King offers her thanks to her husband, Steve King, for his steady support, and her children, Janna and Michelle, who have been lots of fun throughout the making of this book as well as an inspiring source of information about the process of social growth. She also expresses her appreciation to her parents, Marv and Marian Polewach, for having taught her much about showing respect for the individual child and family. Dan Kirschenbaum expresses his appreciation to his wife, Laura Humphrey, and his children, Alexander and Maxwell, for making participation in social growth a thoroughly fascinating and enjoyable experience.

CONTENTS

Preface

1

Introduction 1

2

Three Perspectives on Children's Social Adjustment: Social Learning, Developmental, and Individual Differences 6

3

Forerunners: An Overview of Major Early Intervention Efforts 20

Helping Young Children
Develop Social Skills

1

INTRODUCTION

- ❏ Jeremy bullies the other children on the playground, takes toys from their school lockers, and loses his temper when he doesn't get his way.
- ❏ Erika usually plays alone on the playground and is afraid to approach or join other children.
- ❏ Michael doesn't say anything to his teachers or the lunchroom aides, but other children often take advantage of him by cutting in front of him in line, taking his lunch box desserts, and pouring milk on his lunch tray.
- ❏ Children have complained to the teacher that Jennifer is "mean" and is "always saying things" that hurt their feelings.

These children are having what can be called social adjustment problems. Such problems are not necessarily extreme, nor are they signs of "mental illness." Nevertheless, they can result in unhappiness, rejection, or isolation, and they can have serious, lasting consequences. Our intent in writing this book was to offer mental health professionals some new practical ideas on how to empower children to overcome these problems and avoid such negative outcomes.

OVERALL PURPOSE AND SCOPE

Whether you are a mental health professional (counselor, psychologist, psychiatrist, social worker), a student in training, or a paraprofessional who works with young elementary school children, this book is designed as a guidebook to help you. It has two primary goals. The first is to emphasize the nature and importance of social development and social adjustment among young elementary school children. The second goal is to help you identify children with social adjustment problems and conduct a complete intervention program.

First, we will define social adjustment and describe why it is an important area of focus for persons who work with young elementary school children. In Chapter 2, we will discuss three perspectives on social adjustment. Understanding and applying developmental, social learning, and individual differences perspectives helps us as mental health professionals to avoid the commonly made mistake of teaching specific social skills or behaviors in some automated fashion, as if the goal is to create a community of children who all behave the same way. We will concentrate instead on the primary developmental tasks of young elementary school children and the changing nature of their social thoughts and behaviors. We will also identify some healthy individual differences in the ways elementary school children approach social situations and relate to other children. We emphasize the importance of respecting the uniqueness and special qualities of each child as an individual and this emphasis remains a focus throughout the book.

Chapter 3 describes the major previous early intervention efforts for elementary school children with social adjustment problems. These include the Primary Mental Health Project (PMHP), behaviorally oriented social skills training approaches, and interpersonal cognitive problem-solving approaches. Each of these efforts contributed in some way to the development of the program presented in this book. Although this chapter is a bit more academic and research oriented, the material is presented for those readers who desire more information on related types of programs and sources of additional information on early intervention programs.

Chapter 4 introduces the Social Growth Program for Young Children. This chapter describes the program's overall goals and rationale. The program has the following aims:

- Teach children social skill concepts or *knowledge* through verbal instruction and modeling
- Enhance children's actual behavioral *skills* through rehearsal or practice
- Increase *performance*, or the likelihood of children's using new knowledge and skills through positive feedback
- Enhance the *generalization* of new skills to other settings using FOR ME homework assignments and FOR MY PARENTS AND TEACHERS summary papers that describe session activities.

The program itself has a structured format of nine social skill modules that can be used with individual children or groups of children. Each social skill module begins with a description of its purpose or goals and the rationale for teaching the skill, then offers specific preparation ideas and detailed information on introducing and modeling the social skill. Chapter 4 closes with general guidelines for building good working relationships with children and enhancing the generalization of new skills to school and home settings.

Chapter 5 describes general schoolwide and individual referral systems that target children for early intervention services. Individual assessment methods (interview, observation, rating scales) are discussed as they pertain to the identification of social competencies and adjustment problems. This assessment information makes it possible for you to formulate individualized social growth goals as well as an individualized intervention program. A list of possible goal statements is included as a guide for designing an individualized program. A case example is presented to help you follow the assessment process from screening and referral through the development of an intervention program. The assessment information is analyzed in terms of developmental, social learning, and individual differences perspectives. Finally, the chapter describes the research evaluation of the Wisconsin Early Intervention Program, which provided a basis for developing the Social Growth Program.

Chapter 6 is an extended chapter that presents the nine social skills modules included in the Social Growth Program. These modules cover the following topics:

- **Who Am I?**
  (Emphasizes each child as a unique, growing person.)
- **Who Are We? What Are Social Skills?**
  (Emphasizes the meaning of social skills and importance of getting along with others.)
- **Active Listening**
  (Introduces children to the importance of listening carefully to others and teaches them how to listen carefully.)
- **Warm Messages**
  (Describes how our messages or words affect others and teaches children how to give warm or positive messages.)
- **Asking Questions**
  (Teaches the importance of asking questions when children are confused or afraid and helps children learn how to ask these questions.)
- **Sharing Feelings**
  (Teaches children how to identify emotions and feelings of others and helps children learn the importance of empathy to friendship making.)

- **Standing Up for Me**
  (Teaches children their rights to be safe, to voice some complaints, and to refuse some requests as well as how to voice these rights.)
- **Self-Control**
  (Teaches children the importance of self-control and helps them learn improved self-control.)
- **Social Problem Solving**
  (Teaches children to solve interpersonal problems effectively by considering alternatives and their consequences.)

Chapter 7 presents information on recruiting and selecting paraprofessional group leaders. A recommended training program, along with possible supervision arrangements, is outlined and discussed.

NATURE AND SIGNIFICANCE OF SOCIAL ADJUSTMENT

A socially adjusted elementary school child is accepted by peers and has friends. This child has developed at least one positive, reciprocal relationship with another same-age child. Some socially adjusted children have many friends and are very active and outgoing. Other socially adjusted children have a couple of good, close friendships and are quieter socially or less outgoing. What they have in common is the ability to enjoy the company of others in a positive, socially appropriate way.

Correlates of Social Adjustment

A substantial body of research indicates that social adjustment is an important part of growing up. When children are not popular or accepted by their peers, they tend to struggle in many areas of their lives. Ratings by peers (i.e., sociometric measures) reveal that poorly accepted children have more learning, achievement, and interpersonal problems than their more popular or better accepted peers (Amidon & Hoffman, 1965; Bonney, 1971; Buswell, 1953; Cassidy & Asher, 1989).

Peer acceptance has been related to observed, friendly behaviors (Hartup, Glazer, & Charlesworth, 1967; Marshall and McCandless, 1957). Similarly, Gottman, Gonso, and Rasmussen (1975) found that popular elementary school children distributed and received more positive reinforcement in the classroom than did unpopular children. These groups of children also differed in their knowledge of how to make friends and in their performance on a communication task. In a detailed analysis of children's behaviors, Putallaz and Gottman (1981) observed that unpopular children tend to disagree and call attention to themselves when they join a group of children. Cassidy and Asher (1989) noted that rejected, not neglected, children report the most loneliness. Lonely children tended to behave more aggressively, more disruptively, or in a more withdrawn fashion than other children. Taken together, the data indicates that children who are not well accepted by other children, particularly children who are actively rejected or disliked, tend to experience more social and academic problems than other children.

Social Maladjustment and Problems Over Time

We can all recall socially maladjusted children from our youth. Many of us wonder, "Whatever happened to that strange kid, Bob [or Carol or Ted or Alice or?]?" Not surprisingly, these "odd" or unpopular children, compared with their peers, tend to drop out of school more frequently (Ullman, 1957), exhibit more juvenile delinquency (Roff, Sells, & Golden, 1972), receive more bad conduct discharges from the military (Roff, 1961), and experience more mental health problems in adulthood (e.g., Cowen, Pederson, Babigian, Izzo, & Trost, 1973; Strain, Cooke, & Appolloni, 1976). The negative reputations of unaccepted, rejected children become increasingly entrenched and harder to change across the elementary years. These children become more and more socially segregated from others (Rogosch & Newcomb, 1989). Because a child's behavior is more likely to become consistent with the child's reputation than the reverse (Yarrow & Campbell, 1963), it is obviously desirable for us, as mental health practitioners, to address children's social problems as early as possible.

Peer acceptance during the elementary school years is certainly *not* determined solely by a child's interpersonal behaviors. Children can become unpopular because they look less beautiful than others (Young & Cooper, 1944), because they have uncommon first names (McDavid & Harari, 1966), or because they are black in a white neighborhood or white in a black neighborhood (Singleton & Asher, 1977). Nevertheless, social or interpersonal behaviors are certainly influential to the process of making and keeping friends. Also, children can learn to improve their social behaviors regardless of such virtually inalterable facts of life as physical attractiveness. This book is dedicated to helping children change what they can about the way they relate to others and the way they encourage others to relate to them. Its goal is empowerment and its attitude is unabashedly optimistic: we want to help children learn what they *can do* to improve their social competence.

2

THREE PERSPECTIVES ON SOCIAL ADJUSTMENT:
Social Learning, Developmental, and Individual Differences

THE VALUE OF THREE PERSPECTIVES

Three separate psychological perspectives may help us understand most completely the nature of children's social adjustment problems and how to help reduce them. The *social learning* perspective helps us specify (operationalize) and understand the components of socially competent behavior and the processes by which such behavior is acquired and maintained. A *developmental* perspective helps us identify the nature and development of social behavior during the early elementary school years. This developmental yardstick enables us to set reasonable expectations for our training programs while reminding us that early elementary school children are not little adults; young children *gradually* develop the social and cognitive skills that help them adapt to their increasingly complex worlds. The *individual differences* perspective emphasizes the uniqueness of every child. Each child has a different set of wishes, desires, and expectations that emerge from past experiences; temperamental style; current family, school, and community environments; and the interactions among these factors.

We could attempt to create social development programs that use these three perspectives to impose a rigid model of *a* prototypically socially adapted child. That goal, however, may be neither feasible nor useful. Individual parents, teachers, and mental health professionals have vastly different ideas about the nature of this prototypical child, and participating children have unique backgrounds and individualized ways of approaching new experiences. Our goal is to support each child as a unique person while helping him or her relate to others in ways that are more comfortable and produce more positive outcomes. We do not want to encourage attempts to mold each child into a form that may actually fit only a few.

Let's consider two hypothetical cases that illustrate the importance of an individual differences perspective. Eric, a socially withdrawn boy referred to the intervention program, is a bright, thoughtful, considerate child who shows perseverance and dedication to his favorite hobbies of reading and stamp collecting. Nevertheless, after participation in a social development program, Eric may seem less anxious and more comfortable in the company of his peers. He may always show a preference for quiet solitude and reflection over boisterous social activities, but he may develop a better understanding of his peers' feelings and expectancies and he may learn to communicate with them more effectively. Without giving up his love of solitary activities, Eric may gain a sense of belonging to a peer group and a more positive self-concept than he had before the program.

Susie, on the other hand, is referred to the program because of her bossy, demanding, verbally abusive behavior. A 7-year-old in the second grade, she is beginning to be rejected by her peers, who call her "mean." A look at Susie's strengths reveals that she is very verbal and comfortable taking a leadership role in groups of children. After help in learning to understand other children's feelings, listen to other children, and solve peer conflicts more effectively, Susie is able to become a respected leader of the third-grade soccer team at her school.

Should the program leaders have tried to mold Eric and Susie in the same direction? We think not. Eric seems to have a quiet, reflective temperamental style, with strengths in the areas of perseverance and cognitive abilities. Susie has an active, impulsive temperamental style, with strengths in the areas of verbal and leadership abilities. It may also be the case that Eric and Susie's parents place differing values on these characteristics. Our goals are to support each child's uniqueness and build on each child's strengths. This respect for and encouragement of each child as an individual enhances that child's self-esteem as well as social competence.

A SOCIAL LEARNING PERSPECTIVE

A social learning perspective offers a framework that clearly defines the specific components of adaptive, skillful, or competent social behavior as well as the processes by which such behavior is acquired. This approach is critical to our efforts to help young children with social adjustment problems. It helps us to identify and pinpoint possible problem areas, and it enables us to organize training programs.

Definition of Social Skills and Social Competency

Social skills have been defined as *children's abilities to organize cognitions and behaviors into an integrated course of action directed toward culturally acceptable social or interpersonal goals* (Ladd and Mize, 1983). Thus, social skills refer to social behaviors that are adaptive to, or related to desirable outcomes in, specific situations in one's environment (Mischel, 1973). These social skills are also believed to be acquired, maintained, and changed primarily through learning processes (Bandura & Walters, 1963).

Social competency may be defined as a dynamic, changing *social judgment* regarding a child's social skills in a given situation. Social competency is best considered on a continuum from extremely incompetent to extremely competent. This perspective avoids categorical judgments of "competent" or "incompetent." Instead, it suggests that a child's behavior in a specific situation shows a certain degree or level of competence. Second, competency is not a characteristic that is absolute, engraved in stone, or embodied *within* a child. Rather, competency refers to a social judgment. Thus, one's competency may vary in different cultural settings, in different situations, or when judged by different groups of people. This view argues that understanding the interaction between a child's behaviors and the environment is essential to determining and improving the child's social adjustment.

Components of Socially Competent, Skilled Behavior

What behavioral and cognitive skills and abilities are critical to adaptive and "culturally acceptable" social behaviors? Ladd and Mize (1983) have outlined three component skills, or *skill deficits*, that provide a framework for our conceptualization of component skills. These are:

(1) *Knowledge of Appropriate Social Behavior*

Children may lack knowledge about appropriate social behavior in different situations. What should Julie do if she wants to join a group of girls playing house at the playground structure? What should Sue do if Peter pinches her on the playground? Should Mary sit with a boy in the lunchroom? What kind of clothes do you wear to a birthday party? Norms develop within the peer culture concerning specific behaviors for specific social situations, including dress codes, rules of behavior, vocabulary, and play patterns (e.g., Furman, 1987). Most children seem to develop a cognitive understanding of these norms that guides their social behaviors (e.g., Corsaro, 1981). Ladd and Mize (1983) argue that three types of knowledge about norms are necessary for effective social functioning. These include knowledge of appropriate goals for social interaction, knowledge of appropriate strategies for reaching goals, and knowledge of the situations or contexts within which certain strategies are appropriate. As examples, children may act in ways that discourage peer acceptance if they enter into a game situation with the sole goal of winning the game (Asher & Renshaw, 1981; Renshaw & Asher, 1982) or if they lack knowledge of how to get a game started or of how to join a group of children involved in an activity (e.g., Putallaz & Gottman, 1981).

Consider Jacqueline, an 8-year-old third-grader who has recently moved to Chicago from a rural area in southern Illinois. Jacqueline is having trouble making friends in her new school. A careful assessment of the problem indicates that Jacqueline lacks knowledge about the norms for behavior in her new school. She is seen as a bit "odd" or "different" because she dresses in a "funny way" and doesn't know the school rules about tattling and the kids' unspoken rules about how you join a group of kids.

(2) *Performance of Appropriate Social Behavior*

Some children have a knowledge and cognitive understanding of appropriate social behaviors, but they do not act accordingly. They may be able to explain to peers or younger brothers and sisters how to make a new friend or how to resolve an argument. Faced with the real-world circumstances, however, these children may "freeze" and fail to respond, may respond awkwardly, or may overreact with an excess of behaviors.

Let's consider an example. Sam and Johnny are playing a board game and it's Sam's turn to roll the dice and move his playing piece. Johnny takes Sam's turn out of turn, perhaps unintentionally. Sam immediately shoves Johnny's hand off the board and sends all the pieces flying across the room. Questioned about the incident, Sam is able to explain what he wishes he had done—just casually remind Johnny that it was his turn. What happened? Sam was angry and acted immediately, without thinking. He knows what he should have done but fails to act accordingly when angered in a conflict situation.

Jeffrey also knows how he should handle this kind of common conflict. Unlike Sam, however, Jeffrey doesn't do or say anything when Johnny takes his turn out of turn. This may not be a problem at first, but Johnny begins to cheat intentionally and repeatedly when playing with Jeffrey. Jeffrey feels anxious and afraid of doing or saying anything. He also lacks the ability to respond adaptively in a peer conflict situation.

(3) *Self-monitoring*

Most young elementary school children have developed some ability to take note of their own behavior and its effects on others. When children are able to monitor their behaviors, they are able to learn from their successes and failures. These children give themselves feedback or information about the effects of their behaviors on others. They can use this information to guide their future responses in similar social situations.

Let's consider the ability of Susan, a third-grader, to monitor her own behaviors. Susan complimented Jennifer on her fine playing during the soccer game. Susan noticed that Jennifer smiled, walked back to the car with her, and talked to her about the soccer game at school the next day. But Susan also told Katy that Katy's team lost because she had missed an easy goal. Susan noticed that Katy became very quiet, went home alone, and didn't speak to her the next day. What did Susan learn? Perhaps she learned that her criticism hurt Katy's feelings and that it's hard to keep friends if you criticize them unjustly.

Acquisition and Maintenance of Socially Skilled Behavior

The processes by which children acquire, develop, and maintain social skills have been categorized in various ways by social learning theorists (e.g., Combs & Slaby, 1978; Ladd and Mize, 1983). These categorizations converge, however, in emphasizing four basic learning principles:

(1) *Modeling*

Children learn through observation and imitation. They observe and learn from their parents, teachers, relatives, friends, and neighbors. They also learn from unfamiliar children and adults. These may be children they see playing at the park or adults they see standing in line at the movie theater. A child can also learn from children and adults that he observes on television or at the movies.

Research indicates that children are most likely to model the behaviors of others whom they consider admirable, powerful, or similar to themselves. This is particularly true if the children see the other person reinforced for what he or she does (Bandura, 1977). Many of us have observed small children imitating the behaviors of powerful and, sometimes, admirable television and movie characters (e.g., Superman, Batman, Michaelangelo, Donatello) who win the battles and find the jewels or rescue the "good guys." Although we might be hard pressed to see how the Teenage Mutant Ninja Turtles are similar to our young children or students, they certainly share a love for pizza, adventure, and rowdy games. It is apparent that children can learn aggressive, selfish behaviors from these characters, but we have also observed these same children imitate admirable and respected parents or teachers by reading stories to a pretend classroom or discussing how someone else might share and cooperate with them.

Finally, children also learn from models who are similar to themselves and whom they respect, same-age children who are accepted by their peers.

A child new to a classroom or school may observe and learn a great deal about accepted styles of dress, classroom rules, and popular playground games from these other accepted children.

(2) *Verbal Instruction or Coaching*

Adults and peers teach many social skills through language. They communicate rules, prompts, requests, and directions to help children improve their social adjustment. Classroom *rules* are usually posted in kindergarten classrooms. They may state a list of "Nos" like "No Hitting," "No Yelling," "No Name Calling." These rules teach young children that physical and verbal aggression are not socially acceptable in our society. *Prompts* are commonly used among parents of young children who are in the process of learning how to maneuver in a social world. Common prompts include "What do you say [to your friend whose favorite transformer you just broke]?" or "How can we solve this [to three neighborhood children who want to try out Sarah's new computer game at the same time]?"

(3) *Operant Conditioning*

Complex behaviors, such as those involved in social exchanges, are clearly affected by contingencies. A child learns that a given social behavior produces a given response and then performs the behavior to obtain that response. Julie learns that if she smiles and says "please," Jessica will give her one of her lunchbox treats. Mark learns that if he makes faces and funny noises, his classmates will laugh. Sometimes this learning occurs naturally, without intentional training or intervention. Social behaviors like sharing, complimenting, and helping tend to have positive outcomes that naturally reinforce them.

Children cannot receive contingent reinforcement, however, unless they first perform desirable behaviors. Thus, children who have not learned how to share, compliment, or help others will benefit from initial guidance and direction or modeling prior to the application of contingencies. In *shaping*, a technique that is used to help children perform a new behavior, a child's behavior is compared to some standard or outcome criterion. Positive feedback (praise, approval, tangible reward) is given when the child makes a positive step toward more competent or skillful behavior. For instance, Mark is in the third grade and is still unable to handle group assignments appropriately. His art teacher has recently assigned all of the children to groups with the task of creating their own papier-maché dinosaur. She realizes that in the past Mark has refused to share supplies and has disassembled other group members' efforts. She decides to have her classroom aide shape Mark's behavior by praising each small step (e.g., setting scissors on table, passing scissors to group member) Mark takes toward cooperative group involvement. It is also possible for a child to observe his own behavior and offer himself evaluative feedback. Mark, for example, could keep a tally of his own efforts toward group cooperation and reward himself accordingly.

(4) *Rehearsal*

Parents and teachers sometimes have children practice or rehearse appropriate social behaviors. *Rehearsal* is a central component in social skills training programs. Rehearsal of appropriate behaviors such as asking questions, taking turns, or saying no helps children perform these behaviors more readily. When they rehearse these behaviors, they are learning good habits. Rehearsal facilitates the cognitive processing (encoding, memory, retrieval) of socially skillful behavior and may improve the ability to perform socially skillful behaviors.

A DEVELOPMENTAL PERSPECTIVE

Adjustment for 5-year-olds is a very different matter than adjustment for 10-year-olds. A review of the developmental tasks faced by young elementary school children will help us to set appropriate expectations for their social behavior. What is the course of normal or usual social development during the elementary school years, when children's horizons expand to include school, peer group, and community? We will review the usual social knowledge and behaviors of this age group while taking into account normal variations in the rate at which children master new social behaviors.

Elementary school offers new opportunities to experience increasing independence, belonging to peer groups, and competence and mastery to children between the ages of 5 and 11. Although the young child's parents continue to provide the reassuring stability and positive regard essential to healthy development during these years, the child's new challenges are in the realms of school achievement and peer relationships. Many children will move into these realms with the prerequisite skills, attitudes, and flexibility to enjoy and benefit from them. The all-too-common events of school failure and peer rejection, however, can be painful and have lasting consequences.

Changing Peer Relationships

Peer relationships represent one of the most important arenas in the life of an elementary school child. These relationships become increasingly significant across the early and middle childhood years. Two-year-old children have already begun to communicate and play with peers (Hay, 1979), and studies with preschool children indicate that the amount of peer interaction correlates highly with age (Feiring, 1981). Kindergarten children spend more time talking and playing with peers than do toddlers or young preschoolers.

The way that children play with each other also changes during the early childhood years. Older preschool and elementary school children are more likely than younger preschool children to play in a cooperative, reciprocal fashion. During elementary school, cooperative group activities like board games and team sports become both possible and popular. In contrast, young preschool children are much more apt to play alone or alongside others in a parallel fashion. They may play in the sandbox and make their own castle, right next to their "friend's" castle. These younger children will watch each other and perhaps even share a pail or shovel. But they are much less likely to cooperate in achieving some goal than are elementary children.

Most elementary school children enjoy the company of their peers and form friendships, usually with others of the same sex. Peer group acceptance and a "best friend" enhance a child's sense of importance and competence. These peer contacts also play an important role in children's increasing knowledge of the explicit and implicit rules that guide social behaviors. Most groups of children develop a shared vocabulary and a noticeable degree of conformity in style of dress. An understood dress code for young elementary girls, for example, might be big t-shirts and stretch pants. A girl who arrived in a starched red plaid dress might be seen as "different" and less acceptable. Rules of behavior also characterize children's groups. These might include rules about what it's okay to tell a teacher—that, for example, it might be okay to tell Mrs. Blackburn that Sam hit John but not that Sam called John a "baby."

Sex differences in children's clothes, play patterns, and friends become increasingly apparent as children cross the elementary school years (Furman, 1987). Same-sex friendships are most common among children of this age. Elementary school girls usually play with other girls on the playground and sit with other girls in the lunchroom; elementary school boys usually play with other boys on the playground. These unspoken rules may be situationally specific. They do not necessarily apply in home neighborhoods, where children often play with the next-door neighbor without regard to gender.

Children's understandings of friendships and ideas about friendship change as they get older. Early friendships tend to be momentary and unstable, with fights occurring over toys and space rather than personal feelings (Selman, 1976). These friendships are quickly formed and quickly broken because a friend is simply another child with whom one plays (Damon, 1977). During elementary school, reciprocal exchanges and concrete acts of kindness become increasingly important to friendships. Reciprocal exchanges might include exchanging birthday presents, loaning each other favorite toys, and agreeing to choose each other for partners in school projects. Youniss and Volpe (1978) have also documented the importance of shared rules of conduct (e.g., sharing, "being nice," playing together) among young elementary school friends. Similar information has been obtained from analyses of children's written descriptions of friendship (Bigelow and LaGaipa, 1975).

Developing Cognitive Abilities and Changing Social Behaviors

Cognitive-developmental theorists emphasize the importance of children's changing cognitive structures and abilities during the elementary school years. Elementary school children are more logical and less egocentric in their thinking than preschool children and they seem to become increasingly better at taking another's point of view during the elementary years. These characteristics have major implications for children's ability to maneuver socially.

Consider a kindergarten child, Sarah, who wants to play with the teddy bear that Dianna brought to school for show-and-tell. Dianna is holding onto her bear very tightly. If Sarah can take Dianna's point of view, she might realize that Dianna loves her teddy bear and is afraid that she might lose it at school. Sarah could say something nice about the teddy bear and promise to give it back in just a few minutes. Or consider an interpersonal conflict. Mark and Maria, two first-graders, both want to be first in the lunch line. If these children can talk with each other and learn each other's reason for wanting to be first, they might be able to resolve their conflict. Perhaps Mark wants first choice of desserts and Maria wants first choice of lunchroom seats. Clearly, a child who is trying to persuade someone, cooperate with someone, obtain additional information from someone, or resolve an interpersonal conflict will have an easier time reaching her goal if she can anticipate the other's needs. This child can anticipate reactions and possible objections.

Piaget and Inhelder (1969) emphasized the importance of *how* children think and outlined changes in children's ways of thinking (cognitive structures) across development. They identified a preoperational stage of development for preschool children, during which their judgments are dominated by perceptions. These children usually attend to only one dimension or attribute of an object at a time. They may, for example, notice the height of a glass but not its width. They may notice the size of an object but not its weight. Mastery of more logical ways of thinking, the stage of concrete operational thinking, generally takes place in the elementary school years. During these years, children begin to consider things simultaneously and relate various dimensions of objects, persons, or situations. They become less heavily influenced by superficial appearances and egocentric ideas and increasingly capable of logical thinking.

These logical thinking skills are not reserved solely for mathematics or language problems. Social cognition—that is, the cognitive understanding of oneself, other persons, and the rules of one's society—also improves in many ways across the elementary school years (Shantz, 1982). Piaget conceptualized the relationship between cognitive and social spheres as one of parallelism between cognitive structures and levels of social development. Theoreticians differ, however, in their views of whether the cognitive changes are necessary precursors to changes in social behavior (e.g., Kohlberg, 1969; Schaffer, 1971) or whether social experiences facilitate transitions in cognitive development (e.g., Cairns, 1979). Nevertheless, it is clear that the child's development is best understood within the context of a social environment.

As children grow older, they become increasingly aware of the variety of social roles that an individual can fulfill (e.g., teacher and parent, father and grandfather) (Watson, 1984). They also become less likely to cling to strong sex role stereotypes (Archer, 1984; Stoddart and Turiel, 1985). In addition, they become better able to recognize and avoid using offensive statements (e.g., "You're too fat") (Johnson, Greenspan, & Brown, 1984). Other normal or expected changes during the elementary school years relate to children's increasing ability to recognize others' personality characteristics as they become able to anticipate how these characteristics might affect someone's behavior in any given social situation. These skills have been related to children's ability to resolve conflicts and make friendships (Gottman, 1983).

Children's understanding of themselves also develops at a fast pace during the elementary school years. As children grow, they are more likely to explain their actions in terms of their personality characteristics and feelings rather than solely in terms of external events (Higgins, 1981). They also become better able to view themselves in several dimensions— that is, rather than believing they are "good" or "bad," "smart" or "dumb," they become increasingly aware of their varying strengths and weaknesses (Harter, 1983).

Sometimes a child's self-esteem diminishes at the same time as his self-understanding develops. Some children become more aware of their own shortcomings and are more apt to blame themselves, rather than others or external events, for their mistakes (e.g., Powers and Wagner, 1984). Girls are especially likely to blame themselves for shortcomings (Stipek, 1984). Overall, evidence indicates that self-esteem tends to decrease across the childhood and early adolescent years (Harter, 1983; Savin-Williams and Demo, 1984).

This phenomenon of declining self-esteem highlights the importance of helping children with problems in a major sphere of life, social relationships, as early as possible. Intervention with young children will give them greater opportunities to experience positive social experiences. Children benefit a great deal from successes, especially during this developmental phase of increased self-reflection. Success experiences help them develop feelings of mastery, willingness to attempt new challenges, and positive self-esteem.

AN INDIVIDUAL DIFFERENCES PERSPECTIVE

Although individual differences are, to some extent, addressed by the social learning perspective, we include a separate section here to highlight the importance of working with each child as an individual. Children vary tremendously, depending in part on their genetic make-up and temperamental style; past learning and socialization experiences; and present competencies, expectancies, values, and goals.

Each individual is born with certain biological predispositions that in turn are shaped by experiences across the life span. Documented differences in mood and activity level observed soon after birth (Thomas & Chess, 1977), and data on personality similarities among twins (Buss & Plomin, 1975) suggest the influence of genetic factors. Of course, parents and others also respond differently to infants according to their individual characteristics. A reciprocal exchange of influence begins immediately.

Individual differences also arise from unique experiences. These include major and daily life events as well as family structure and ongoing family interaction patterns. Each child encounters a unique set of rewards and punishments at home, at school, and in the neighborhood. Moreover, role models that are available and attractive in each child's environment will play a role in developing personal styles or individual differences.

The behaviors of many children whom we have known for a long time seem to be somewhat predictable. Statements like "Johnny's like that" or "Mary always does that in a new situation" or "We should have guessed that Sam would act out with a substitute teacher" reflect our beliefs that some individual characteristics among children are stable. Although we are sometimes surprised by children's behaviors, we tend to see some constancy in a child's behavior across situations.

Eysenck (1981) has described three primary personality factors, introversion-extroversion, neuroticism (emotional stability-instability), and psychoticism (contact with reality), which are relatively stable, characteristic ways of perceiving and responding that Eysenck believes have their basis in physiology. One of these factors, introversion-extroversion, has been documented in many factor-analytic studies and is most relevant to our discussion of individual differences in social behavior.

Introversion-extroversion concerns the extent to which a person's orientation is turned outward toward the external world or inward toward the self. Characteristics associated with introversion are introspective, risk-avoidant behaviors. Characteristics associated with extroversion are sociable, impulsive, thrill-seeking behaviors. Although these characteristics tend to be moderately stable across adolescence and adulthood (e.g., Conley, 1985), many individuals do change these attributes dramatically across the life span. Thus, a child's personal style or level of extroversion should always be considered but not taken as an absolute or inalterable characteristic.

Let's consider how a child's interpersonal style, or orientation toward the world, might affect her social behaviors within an intervention program. A child who tends to avoid risks and be introspective might need more time to establish a feeling of comfort and trust within the group setting. This sense of personal comfort may be a prerequisite to trying out new social behaviors. On the other hand, a child who is outgoing and impulsive may barge fearlessly into new situations. This same child may require redirection in the group and help slowing down to consider the consequences of impulsive behaviors.

Social learning theory emphasizes the interaction between the personal determinants of behavior and the situational or environmental determinants of behavior. This perspective assumes that a child's actions in a given situation vary with the situation, with his appraisal of the situation, and with his past experiences in similar situations. For instance, a child may behave in similar ways in a math class and a reading class, in which the expectancies for children's behavior may be similar; the child may also have similar values and goals for her performance in these two situations. On the other hand, this same child may behave totally differently while playing in the neighborhood after school. The community's expectancies for children's after-school play behavior are probably very different from classroom expectancies. A child's own cognitive appraisal of the situation is also likely to be different.

Personal determinants of behavior reflect differences in children's past experiences and present capabilities. These are referred to as *person variables* (Mischel, 1973), five of which are:

(1) *Competencies: What Can You Do?*

These include intellectual abilities, social skills, physical skills, and other special skills and abilities. Does the child know how to answer the telephone or greet a new friend? Is the child able to remember other children's names? Is the child able to ride a bike with the other children?

(2) *Encoding Strategies: How Do You See It?*

Children differ in the way they selectively attend to information from the environment, encode events, and store information in meaningful categories. When a child sees a "friend" pick up his tray and move to a different lunch table, does the child encode this as rejection, an indication of the other child's disloyalty, an indication that the other child might not be feeling well, or something else? When a child is rewarded with a star on a math paper, does the child encode that as a personal achievement or a reflection of the teacher's low standards?

(3) *Expectancies: What Will Happen?*

Expectancies concerning the consequences of behaviors often guide the choice of behaviors. Does the child expect that sharing will be reciprocated? Does the child expect to be caught cheating? Does the child expect hard work at school to be acknowledged by parents?

(4) *Subjective Values: What Is It worth?*

Children value outcomes differently and may choose to behave differently in accord with these values. Does the child place a high value on pleasing the teacher or obtaining a certain child's friendship?

(5) *Self-Regulatory Systems and Plans: How Can You Achieve It?*

Children differ in the self-imposed rules and standards for regulating their own behavior. They may reward themselves for certain successes and they may set priorities and make plans for reaching a goal.

Summary

Children vary tremendously in how they perceive and respond in a given social setting. Some of these differences may be fleeting, but many of them reflect stable perceptual tendencies and response patterns. These differences have their roots in genetic predispositions and several years of learning experiences. In our complex social world, a number of responses can be appropriate and adaptive in a given situation; that is, many of these individual differences represent healthy differences that contribute to the interesting, lively variety of persons in our world. Some of these differences, however, present maladaptive response patterns. Although these patterns may be somewhat stable, they are not necessarily permanent. The intervention program described in this book is designed to alter maladaptive response patterns so that children may relate to others more easily and enjoy more positive outcomes than were previously available to them.

AN INTEGRATION OF PERSPECTIVES: A CASE CONCEPTUALIZATION

Let's consider how these three perspectives contribute to our understanding of Eric, the extremely withdrawn 6-year-old first-grader first mentioned in this chapter's introduction. His teacher reports that Eric has not spoken in the classroom and has no friends; he sits alone in the lunchroom and plays alone on the playground. Eric's mother says that she is very worried about Eric because he hasn't made any friends in the neighborhood and spends most of his time reading, collecting stamps, and watching television.

The *social learning* perspective enables us to pinpoint the components of socially appropriate behavior that represent problems for Eric. A thorough assessment might indicate that he has a good cognitive understanding of the informal rules of behavior for children within the school and of how to make friends. The assessment also indicates that Eric would like to have a friend, although he places a higher value on maintaining his hobbies of stamp collecting and reading *(subjective values)*. He often misinterprets other children's intentions *(cognitive encoding error)* and expects that any effort that he makes to speak or play with another child will fail *(expectancies)*. He tends to become anxious and "freeze" when near an unfamiliar child or a group of children *(performance problem)*.

The *developmental* perspective enables us to consider common or usual patterns of peer acceptance and friendship during elementary school. Strong, active peer friendships are both common during elementary school and associated with positive adjustment in many areas. These friendships are usually less egocentric than preschool friendships. They offer elementary school children a sense of belonging and an important arena within which to learn about themselves, others, and social rules. They may involve reciprocal exchanges of information or belongings and concrete acts of kindness.

The *individual differences* perspective stresses the importance of supporting Eric as an important individual who has his own set of life experiences. He has his own preferences, values, and goals, and these should be respected. We learn from our assessment that Eric is a bright, considerate child who tends to be a bit introspective. He avoids risks and describes a preference for quiet, solitary activities. Nevertheless, Eric reports that he would like to have a friend with whom to share some activities at home and at school. But he perceives other children, including unfamiliar children, as being hostile and mean. He expects that any exchanges with these children will result in feelings of sadness or anger.

A careful integration of information gathered from the three perspectives enables us to help Eric in a sensitive and sensible way. Eric may always show a preference for quiet solitude and studious activities, but we can help him to alter inaccurate expectancies and misinterpretations regarding other children's behaviors. We can also help Eric become more at ease in social situations. These positive changes may help Eric develop some desired friendships and a sense of belonging to the very social world of elementary school children.

3

FORERUNNERS:
An Overview of Early Intervention Efforts

The intervention program described in this book was based on our own program experiences; our beliefs about the value of combining social learning, developmental, and individual differences perspectives; and the past work of many other mental health professionals and researchers. Accordingly, let us now briefly survey some of the guiding and forerunner program efforts as a framework for understanding the goals and rationale of the intervention methods to be described in subsequent chapters.

There have been many efforts to prevent or reduce social adjustment problems among elementary school children. Although the overall focus of these efforts is on helping young children relate to others in ways that are more socially adaptive and less personally distressing, intervention methods have differed. In this section, we will review secondary prevention programs that are child focused. By *secondary prevention*, we mean early intervention efforts with children at risk—that is, children who are exhibiting maladaptive social behaviors that have recently been detected and are not severe enough to warrant intensive therapy or residential treatment. Our emphasis will also be on *child-focused* programs that work directly with children, individually or in small groups, to develop their self-esteem, social competencies, and/or level of comfort in social situations. Although this review will necessarily be somewhat selective, we will examine several major early intervention efforts and research on their effectiveness.

THE PRIMARY MENTAL HEALTH PROJECT (PMHP)

The Primary Mental Health Project (PMHP) is a school-based early identification and intervention program that has been operational, in varying forms, for 30 years (Cowen, Trost, Lorion, Dorr, Izzo, & Isaacson, 1975). Through annual workshops and extensive publication, PMHP serves as a national model and has clearly influenced many early intervention programs (Cowen, Spinell, Wright, & Weissberg, 1983). Initiated as a pilot demonstration program in a single school in Rochester, New York, PMHP has since expanded in the Rochester area as well as nationally and internationally.

In this program identified children are seen individually and in small groups by trained paraprofessionals who are supervised by mental health professionals. Ideally, a warm, supportive, relationship is formed between the child and paraprofessional, and this relationship provides the context within which positive changes can be made.

One major feature of PMHP is its systematic screening and identification of young elementary school children, kindergarten through third grade, who are experiencing adjustment problems. Thus, PMHP uses a proactive approach, seeking to identify children at risk before their problems become severe or entrenched. A second major feature is the altered role of school-based mental health professionals in the program. Rather than exclusively providing direct service or treatment, these mental health professionals serve as trainers and supervisors of paraprofessionals. Given that overall frequency estimates of school adjustment problems range from 20 percent to 30 percent of the school population (e.g., Dohrenwend, Dohrenwend, Gould, Link, Neugebauer, & Wunschhitzig, 1980; Glidewell & Swallow, 1969), the effective use of paraprofessional helpers clearly enhances our ability to address the problems of young children in significant numbers.

Program evaluation studies document PMHP's effectiveness from the perspectives of participating teachers, child aides (i.e., paraprofessionals), and mental health professionals (Cowen, Gesten, & Wilson, 1979; Cowen, Zax, Izzo, & Trost, 1966). More recently, Weissberg, Cowen, Lotyczewski, and Gesten (1983) have described their evaluation of seven consecutive years (1974–75 to 1980–81) of PMHP program services. During these years, the trained paraprofessionals or child aides saw each participating child individually, once or twice weekly, for 30 to 45 minutes. Referral and outcome data include problem and competency behavior rating scales completed by teachers as well as parallel ratings from paraprofessionals and professionals. The findings of Weissberg et al. suggest that children seen through PMHP improved in adjustment according to all three types of raters. The findings also suggest that PMHP was more effective with shy and anxious children than with acting-out, aggressive children. Unfortunately, the ratings were all completed by program participants who are, presumably, invested in finding positive gains from their work. It is also the case that this relatively ambitious investigation did not include a control group. Therefore, other factors such as normal developmental changes could have accounted for some of the positive findings.

A short-term follow-up study has suggested that apparent positive gains associated with PMHP services continue (Lorion, Caldwell, & Cowen, 1976), and, reporting on a relatively long-term follow-up study of PMHP services, Chandler, Weissberg, Cowen, and Guare (1984) document the endurance of some positive changes over time. A group of children who obtained PMHP services two to five years earlier was compared to a demographically similar group of peers who never obtained PMHP services and to a demographically similar group of poorly adjusted children. Teacher ratings of children's problems and competencies, children's self-reports of competencies, and academic achievement scores were collected. Although groups did not differ systematically on academic achievement and self-report variables, teacher ratings revealed that the PMHP group was significantly better adjusted than the current poorly adjusted children, although not as well adjusted as the other group of children. In addition, the PMHP group seemed to maintain initial gains; the highest problem ratings occurred at referral and the lowest at follow-up.

In examining the application of PMHP to other school districts, Cowen, Weissberg, Lotyczewski, Bromley, Gilliland-Mallo, DeMeis, Farago, Grassi, Haffey, Weiner, and Woods (1983) describe evaluations of six independent school district PMHP-type programs in New York. Some common measures of outcomes completed by teachers and child aides (paraprofessionals) were used, making it possible to analyze findings across districts. Although control groups were not included and assessments were completed by program staff, findings indicated that each district program was working effectively and that, overall, the "pooled change profile" was strongly positive.

Nevertheless, all evaluations of PMHP programs have not been overwhelmingly positive and glowing. Stein and Polyson (1984), reconsidering PMHP's effectiveness by means of a meta-analysis of controlled empirical studies, noted that effect sizes, based on the assumption of no positive gains for nontreated children, were actually quite small and were obtained inconsistently.

SOCIAL SKILLS TRAINING PROGRAMS

Behaviorally oriented social skills training programs offer a promising approach to dealing with children's social adjustment problems. The distinction between models that are more or less rigorous in their behavioral orientation is a bit fuzzy. Some of the defining aspects of behavioral programs, however, are a situation-specific view of children's skills rather than a cross-situational personality trait view. Behaviorally oriented approaches also emphasize empirical evaluations with clear, operationally defined variables (Kirschenbaum, 1983). Given the increased number of careful empirical investigations of cognitive variables in recent years, we generally include cognitive-behavioral skills training programs within this general category.

The main objective of social skills training programs is to enhance adaptive social behaviors. Most of these programs are based on the deficit hypothesis—that is, that people may lack the skills necessary for appropriate social behavior (McFall, 1976). As we noted in Chapter 1, children's social skills have been defined as their "ability to organize cognitions and behaviors into an integrated course of action directed toward some culturally acceptable social or interpersonal goals" (Ladd & Mize, 1983). In keeping with this definition, social skills training programs emphasize the acquisition and/or modification of specific cognitive and behavioral responses.

The skill deficits that have been addressed by social skills intervention programs were discussed in Chapter 2. These include: (1) a lack of knowledge about appropriate social behavior, (2) a failure to make use of knowledge and perform appropriate social behaviors, and (3) a failure to self-monitor behaviors and their consequences (Ladd & Mize, 1983).

Let's consider a second-grade boy, Jason, who wants to "make friends" with Robert, a boy who was introduced as a new member of Jason's class today. Obviously, there is no single sequence of most appropriate behaviors because, to some extent, the appropriateness of Jason's behaviors would depend on Robert's responses and the nature of the reciprocal exchange that develops between the boys. Nevertheless, we would certainly have greater confidence in Jason's chances of successfully reaching his goal if Jason (1) has knowledge of possible appropriate behaviors, (2) is able to "do" what he "knows" would be appropriate and likely to help in making friends, and (3) is sensitive to feedback on the effects that his behaviors have on Robert and on his developing friendship with Robert.

Two key elements of adaptive social behavior addressed by social skills training programs are *knowledge* and *skilled performance*. A child must have knowledge of appropriate social or interpersonal behaviors. Of equal if not greater importance, however, is the ability to translate that knowledge into skilled performance. Most social skills programs include training methods designed to provide knowledge and enhance performance. Some programs also focus on a third important element, the *generalization* of new skills to nontraining settings such as home, classroom, and playground.

The primary training methods used in these social skills training programs include verbal or modeled instruction, rehearsal, and feedback (Ladd & Mize, 1983). A number of studies have been conducted using one or a combination of these methods. For illustrative purposes, we will focus on some of the most effective programs designed for improving the social skills or social competencies of elementary school children.

Early empirically evaluated social skills training efforts are perhaps best represented by the work of Oden and Asher (1977). Oden and Asher sought to improve the social skills and peer relationships of third- and fourth-grade children who scored relatively low on peer acceptance. The four social skills they focused on were participation, cooperation, communication, and validation/support. Within a short, five-session program, they described each skill verbally and offered examples; included time for behavioral rehearsal or practice; and offered feedback, discussed progress, and reviewed instructions. Compared to a group of elementary children who did not participate in the program, participants showed gains in sociometric play ratings or peer acceptance that were maintained at the one year follow-up.

Ladd (1981) designed and evaluated a social skills training program aimed at improving the peer interactions and acceptance of third grade children. Program participants had low peer acceptance ratings and infrequently used three social skills: asking questions of peers, leading peers, and offering supportive statements to peers. The program included verbal instructions to promote an understanding of the skill and thereby promote children's knowledge about appropriate social behavior. It also included guided rehearsal, in which the children tried performing the behaviors accompanied by informative feedback. These training methods were used to increase behavioral skill and performance. Finally, in an effort to facilitate the maintenance and generalization of social-behavioral gains, self-directed rehearsal and evaluation were included. This program resulted in significant increases in sociometric status or peer acceptance for program participants compared to an attention control group and a nontreatment control group. Gains in asking questions of peers and leading peers were also documented for program participants.

Michelson, Sugai, Wood, and Kazdin (1983) designed another systematic program to improve social skills. This program offered sixteen "modules" that focused on assertive behavior, which can be defined as honest, fair, direct expressions of self that do not put down or violate the rights of others. Topics covered by the modules included, among others, giving and receiving compliments, making complaints, saying no, and standing up for personal rights. A standard training format was used for each module that included a lecture or verbal instruction on the usefulness of a new skill, modeling between trainers, modeling between trainers and children, and modeling between children. Behavioral rehearsal (practice) with feedback and homework assignments between sessions were also used. Michelson, Mannarino, Marchione, Stein, Figueroa, and Beck (1983) found that this program was more effective in improving social skills than a cognitive–problem-solving program, a Rogerian approach, or no training.

One of the more systematically evaluated large-scale programs was the Social Skills Development Program (SSDP) that provided services to hundreds of young inner city children in Cincinnati (Kirschenbaum, Pedro-Carroll, & DeVoge, 1983). The foundation of SSDP can be traced to the Primary Mental Health Project (PMHP), and Kirschenbaum, one of the authors of this book, served as the SSDP research director during its early years. SSDP made use of trained paraprofessionals, mass screening procedures to identify children at risk, and school-based services. In keeping with a social competence model, SSDP attempted to emphasize positive growth and minimize the stigma and negative attitudes associated with a traditional mental health model. Innovative features of SSDP included its focus on specific social skills and its provision of services within small, structured groups. As described in Kirschenbaum (1979), children received an average of 27 group sessions that usually included: (1) group discussion, (2) structured activities designed to improve specific, targeted social skills, (3) free-play activities, (4) clean-up, (5) snacks, contingent on following group rules, and (6) wrap-up discussions. SSDP used methods of instruction, modeling, and contingency management to improve skills such as differentiation of feelings and interpersonal problem solving.

In studies conducted between 1975 and 1977 on the effectiveness of SSDP (Kirschenbaum, Pedro-Carroll, & DeVoge, 1983), children in direct social skills intervention groups and children who obtained indirect consultation services improved significantly more than controls in teacher-rated social competence. In addition, 92 percent of teachers who received SSDP consultation rated services in the "somewhat helpful" to "very helpful" range. One of the teachers commented, "It was successful with 80 percent of the children in my class who benefited either from therapy or consultation. The consultations were about the only thing that got me through the year." Another teacher said, "[The SSDP staff] are a great help when you get down. They are terrific listeners. They really stress positive points, never condemn. They give constructive criticism." Observational data indicated that children who obtained social skills training increased their frequency of cooperative interactions with teachers more than children in consultation and control groups did. Although teachers did not report changes in problem behaviors as a function of intervention and some of the findings were mixed, the overall evidence suggests that the social skills approach was a low-cost, proactive, positive approach to promoting children's social adaptation.

More recently, Bierman, Miller, and Stabb (1987) evaluated the effectiveness of a social skills training program for elementary school boys who were disliked by their peers and showed high rates of negative social behaviors. These boys were randomly assigned to one of the following treatment conditions: (1) instructions to promote positive social behavior, (2) prohibitions to decrease negative social behavior, (3) a combination of instructions to promote positive behavior and prohibitions to decrease negative behaviors, and (4) no treatment. Instructions focused on the positive social behaviors of questioning others, helping, and sharing. These findings revealed that boys who received prohibitions and a response-cost consequence (loss of privilege—ability to earn tokens) for negative behavior during play sessions displayed fewer negative behaviors immediately after and six weeks after intervention. Instructions and reinforcement of specific social skills seemed to promote more social initiations and more positive interactions six weeks after treatment. The combination of prohibitions and instructions resulted in immediate decreases in negative behaviors and stable improvements in peer interactions. Finally, only the combination of both prohibitions and instructions resulted in behavioral as well as sociometric improvement. Across a number of studies, it seems that social behavior is more responsive to social skills treatment programs than is peer acceptance.

Although a small-scale program may be limited in generalizability or external validity, this recent effort by Bierman et al. (1987) illustrates the increasing emphasis on identifying the effective treatment components within a social skills training program. Bierman et al. compared instructional efforts aimed at increasing children's social knowledge to a contingency management approach. It would appear from the findings that these components had differing, albeit complementary, positive effects.

INTERPERSONAL COGNITIVE PROBLEM-SOLVING INTERVENTIONS

Another major and related approach for dealing with children's social adjustment problems involves programs that train children in social or interpersonal cognitive problem-solving (ICPS) skills. Although training components aimed at enhancing knowledge or social cognitions were included in some of the social skills programs reviewed in the previous section, the intervention efforts described in this section placed their primary emphasis on interpersonal cognitive problem-solving skills. Spivack and Shure (1974) conceptualize ICPS skills as a group of related skills or abilities that include a sensitivity to human problems, an ability to consider alternative courses of action (alternative thinking), an ability to conceptualize the means to solving a problem or reaching a goal (means-end thinking), and an understanding and sensitivity to the pros and cons or consequences of one's behaviors (consequential thinking). Spivack and Shure also argue that these skills are essential to children's social adjustment and that training and improvement in these skills will improve children's social adaptation. This assumption—that interpersonal cognitive problem-solving skills are associated with children's social competence—is discussed and evaluated in the next section.

ICPS Skills and Social Competence

ICPS skills have been clearly associated with social competence in some groups of children and adolescents (e.g., McKim, Weissberg, Cowen,

Gesten, & Rapkin, 1982; Spivack & Shure, 1982). Shure and Spivack (1972) studied means-end thinking among 10- to 12-year old "disturbed" and normal children. The children were presented with a number of stories involving interpersonal problems. Once again, the "disturbed" or less well-adjusted children were found to use fewer and less adaptive means-end thoughts than the normal children. In a 1974 report, Spivack and Shure noted that well-adjusted preschool children offered more hypothetical solutions to problems and showed a better understanding of the consequences of their actions than did poorly adjusted children.

Nevertheless, positive associations have not always been found between ICPS skills and social competence (e.g., Weissberg, Gesten, Carnrike, Toro, Rapkin, Davidson, & Cowen, 1981), particularly among relatively homogeneous groups of school-age children. Hopper and Kirschenbaum (1985) discovered that limitations in the measurement of children's ICPS skills could account for some of these inconsistent findings. They observed that one common measure—quantity of alternative solutions generated—was unrelated to social competence within a relatively homogeneous group of sixth-grade children. Rather, the child's ability to generate effective solutions consistently was important. This is in keeping with the findings of Richard and Dodge (1982) that socially competent children differ from their incompetent peers in the quality of second solutions they give to resolve interpersonal problems. It seems that the child's ability to generate a small number of high-quality responses is probably more relevant to social adaptation than the ability to generate many responses of mixed quality. If a child can rapidly generate a good response (i.e., act appropriately) when he is kicked by another child, has his turn taken out of turn, or is faced with a failing test grade, he may also have reasonably good peer relationships.

Finally, Denham and Almeida (1987) report findings of meta-analyses assessing the relations among interpersonal cognitive problem-solving skills (ICPS) and behavioral adjustment. They included studies that shared the conceptual premise and variables put forth by Spivack and Shure and that involved subjects between 3 and 12 years of age. Results of the meta-analyses indicated strong support for the notion that ICPS skills differentiate adjusted from maladjusted children. The average adjusted child scored above the 63rd percentile of the nonadjusted group.

ICPS Skills Training Programs

Spivack and Shure have developed a structured program that aims to train young children systematically to use these skills. In these programs a series of scripts and group exercises are used to encourage the development of essential problem-solving thinking processes (Spivack, Platt, & Shure, 1976). A program was originally devised for teachers to use with preschool classes and then revised for kindergarten children (Shure &

Spivack, 1974) and elementary school children (Shure, 1981). Preliminary lessons for each age group focus on language and thinking skills that are considered necessary prerequisites for effective problem solving.

The program for kindergarten children involves prerequisite skills that focus on understanding basic word concepts such as *same-different, if-then, before-after, why-because,* and *now-later.* The problem-solving sections involve the use of problem pictures defined by the teacher's comments. For instance, one picture shows two children in a grocery store with their mother; one of the children is pushing a grocery cart and the other child wants to push the cart (Spivack & Shure, 1974). The children are guided by their teacher, in small groups, who uses the basic word concepts to obtain children's ideas about alternative solutions, alternative consequences, and a pairing of solutions with consequences.

One potential advantage of this approach is that training children to use general thinking processes enables them to apply these ways of thinking to a wide range of social situations. Thus, advocates of ICPS skills training programs argue that these programs address the important need to work toward a generalization of new skills to many different situations.

In initial studies aimed at assessing the effectiveness of ICPS skills training, Spivack and Shure (1974) found positive effects for nursery school and kindergarten inner city black children. Measures of alternative and consequential thinking indicated significant gains for these children when compared to matched no-treatment control groups. Behavioral ratings also offered supporting evidence for the ICPS skills training programs. As an example, although their use of teachers as both program service providers and program evaluators may have introduced some bias into the data, 70 percent of initially maladjusted kindergarten children were judged to have improved following the program as compared to only 6 percent of the maladjusted comparison children.

Nelson and Carson (1988) recently evaluated a social problem-solving skills program for third- and fourth-grade children. They completed an unusually comprehensive assessment of the program by including social skills knowledge and role-play tests, teacher ratings of child behaviors, children's self-reports, and a sociometric measure of peer acceptance. Eighteen lessons covered affective and behavioral skills as well as cognitive problem solving. In two studies, however, significant improvement in knowledge and performance of social problem-solving skills were not accompanied by consistent improvements in behavioral adjustment and peer acceptance.

Durlak (1985) and Pellegrini and Urbain (1985) have reviewed additional empirical evidence for the efficacy of ICPS skills training with children who show some social adjustment problems. It is clear that not all program efforts have had results as beneficial as those reported by Spivack and Shure (1974). As an example, Sharp (1981) included an attention-control group, made an effort to keep teachers "blind" to children's treatment status, and included observational ratings of social behaviors in their assessment. Although nursery school children who participated in their ICPS program made gains in alternative thinking, no gains were found in adjustment ratings or in observed social behaviors. Urbain (1980) compared a behavioral contingency management program to combination programs offering ICPS plus self-instructional training and social perspective taking plus self-instructional training, respectively. Although all interventions were associated with improvement on social-cognitive measures, none of the interventions were associated with improvement on behavioral ratings.

As Durlak (1985) concluded in his review of ten published outcome studies that assessed the impact of training on adjustment, participating children consistently improved in their cognitive problem-solving skills following intervention. This conclusion is also supported by the meta-analyses performed by Denham and Almeida (1987). Durlak (1985), however, argued that Spivack and Shure have been the only investigators to demonstrate a consistent relationship between training and improved social or behavioral adjustment. Although Denham and Almeida asserted that training children to improve social problem-solving has been associated with improvements in behavioral adjustment in some studies, the existing data does not strongly support the view that ICPS skills mediate adjustment.

SUMMARY AND CONCLUSIONS

This chapter described some of the major secondary prevention programs that served as forerunners to the Social Growth Program. These early intervention programs have in common the general goal of enhancing children's social adjustment or adaptation. Consider the two children introduced at the beginning of this book: Erik, who played alone and was afraid or anxious when others were nearby, and, Jennifer, who was verbally abusive toward other children. Children with similar problems have participated in, and perhaps benefited from, each of the programs described in this chapter.

Differences among the programs are apparent when we examine the specific methods they use to reach these goals. The Primary Mental Health Project (PMHP) was a major forerunner in its use of proactive screening to identify children at risk and in its use of trained, supervised paraprofessionals. These two innovations enabled large numbers of children to obtain services before their problems became entrenched. PMHP also emphasized the development of warm, supportive relationships between children and trained paraprofessionals that could provide the context for positive changes.

Some social skills training programs, such as the large-scale Cincinnati Social Skills Development Program (SSDP), built on the PMHP model. These programs placed a greater emphasis on assessing, specifying, and training situation-specific social skills. Interventions in social skills training programs also tend to be structured and clearly defined, with an emphasis on instruction, rehearsal, and feedback. Evaluations of these programs show that children do improve their social behavioral skills in targeted areas. These behavioral improvements, however, are not always associated with changes in peer acceptance.

Programs designed to train children in interpersonal cognitive problem-solving (ICPS) skills are based on the assumption that enhancing children's knowledge or social cognitions will help them in their social and behavioral adaptations. The tendency to generate consistently good solutions to social problems has been associated with social competence. Although children often do improve their problem-solving skills in carefully conducted intervention programs, these changes have not been clearly associated with improved social behavioral adjustment. In short, none of these early intervention approaches stand alone as the only effective or most effective approach. Rather, each has contributed some refreshing ideas and effective techniques for professionals committed to working with young children.

4

THE SOCIAL GROWTH PROGRAM:
An Overview

GOALS AND RATIONALE

The Social Growth Program is an early intervention program designed to help young primary-grade children with social and emotional adjustment problems. It is designed for use by school-based practitioners who may be working with many groups of children as well as private, community-based practitioners working with an individual child or small groups of children. The program was established with the belief that early identification of social adjustment problems and a positive environment for improvement could minimize children's distress, enhance their self-esteem, and minimize the likelihood of their problems worsening and becoming linked with negative peer reputations.

Drawing on the experiences of colleagues involved in PMHP programs, social skills training programs, and ICPS training programs, we designed our program with the goal of providing helpful services to young children with social adjustment problems. Achieving this goal required screening and early identification and the use of trained, supervised paraprofessionals to reach large numbers of children. We also believed a program that offered structured, skills-oriented interventions within the context of warm, supportive relationships would be most effective. These skills-oriented interventions were developed into lesson modules that focus on both social-behavioral and social-cognitive skills.

Although specific goals depend on the individual needs of participating children, broadly speaking these goals fall within the following general categories:

- To teach children social skill concepts or knowledge through verbal instruction and modeling

- To enhance children's actual behavioral social skills through rehearsal or practice
- To increase children's performance or use of new knowledge and skills through positive feedback
- To enhance the generalization of new skills to other settings

We are optimistic about young children's capacities for social and emotional growth and consider each child's adjustment problems within a broader context that also acknowledges their strengths. The avoidance of negative labeling and a pathological bias are crucial to the success of the entire program as well as to the success of individual participants. Children who are likely to benefit from such a program do not have serious, chronic psychiatric disorders that require intensive treatment. Rather, these are children whose temperamental styles, social-cognitive developmental level, and life experiences have combined to place them at some risk for poor interpersonal relationships and secondary problems associated with poor self-esteem and peer rejection or isolation. It is important that an early intervention program maintain its reputation as an educational program that promotes healthy development, not as a mental health service for "disturbed" or "disordered" children.

CONTENT OF SOCIAL GROWTH MODULES

The nine Social Growth Modules can be integrated into an intervention program for individual children or small groups of four or five children. These modules were written after a careful review of current research on teaching social skills to children, and our approach is based on the belief that adaptive interpersonal behaviors can be taught in a systematic, goal-directed manner. Each module includes preparation and presentation ideas for kindergarten through second-grade children as well as third- through fourth-grade children. Both the number and order of modules can be varied according to children's needs. The nine modules and the goals that they address are as follows.

Who Am I?

This is recommended as the first module in any individual or group program. Its primary focus is on building rapport and helping each child feel comfortable and accepted. The module can also be used to address goals that include (1) increasing self-understanding (increase accurate description of physical appearance, skills, abilities, limitations; increase recognition and verbalization of likes and dislikes, increase recognition and verbalization of needs), and (2) enhancing a positive self-image (increase the frequency of realistic, positive statements about self, increase the frequency of maintaining a positive mood when negative feedback or failure experiences occur, increase the frequency of behaviors that require risk taking within a group).

Who Are We? What Are Social Skills?

This module introduces children to the meaning and importance of social skills. They learn that much of what they do each day occurs within a social context and that some interpersonal behaviors evoke more positive outcomes than others. Children are encouraged to identify their existing social skills and consider the importance of these skills in their daily lives. Individual goals that might be addressed include (1) increasing understanding of self (increase accurate description of skills and frequency of positive, realistic statements about self), (2) increasing physical and emotional comfort when others give positive feedback, and (3) increasing understanding of how one's own behaviors affect others.

Active Listening

This module introduces children to the importance of listening carefully to others' messages and offers opportunities to practice listening skills. Along with the first two modules, Active Listening is one of the core modules for most intervention programs. Individualized goals that might be addressed include (1) increasing understanding of other children's feelings and concerns; (2) minimizing confusion about assignments, tasks, and game rules; and (3) improving conversations with others.

Warm Messages

The instructional component of this module focuses on how the types of messages we give affect others. Children learn to distinguish between messages that make people feel "warm" or positive and messages with opposite or "cold" effects. Children are given opportunities to practice giving "warm" messages to each other. Individualized goals that might be addressed include (1) improving understanding of how one's own behaviors affect others, and (2) improving one's ability to get along with others.

Asking Questions

This module instructs children in the importance of asking questions to obtain information when they are confused or afraid. Children are given opportunities to practice different ways of asking questions and observe how others are affected by the way questions are asked. Individualized goals that might be addressed include (1) increasing the frequency of appropriate questions when one is confused about assignments, rules, or tasks or when one is afraid in new situations; (2) increasing understanding

of one's needs; and (3) increasing understanding of how one's own behaviors affect others.

Sharing Feelings

This module instructs children in the importance of empathy in social
exchanges and friendship building and offers them ample opportunity to
practice discriminating and labeling others' emotions. Individualized goals
that might be addressed include: (1) increasing the frequency of recogniz-
ing emotions in others, (2) increasing understanding of how actions affect
others, and (3) improving relationships with others.

Standing Up for Me

This module instructs children in their personal rights to feel safe and
be safe, voice some complaints, and refuse some requests. Children learn
ways to refuse requests or resist situations that may be harmful as well as
the importance of expressing concerns to trusted adults. They also learn
how to express some negative opinions or dissatisfactions in a constructive
way. Individualized goals that might be addressed include: (1) increasing
understanding of personal rights, (2) increasing constructive expression of
dissatisfaction, (3) increasing frequency of refusing inappropriate requests,
and (4) increasing personal feelings of worth and empowerment.

Self-Control

This module instructs children in the importance of learning to
regulate their own behaviors. They learn that self-control helps them
complete assignments, get along better with others, and feel good about
themselves. Children then practice setting personal standards and
monitoring their own performance. Individualized goals that might be
addressed include (1) decreasing distraction and increasing completion of
tasks, (2) increasing frequency of maintaining self-control when faced with
negative feedback from others, (3) increasing positive self-esteem, and (4)
improving relationships with others.

Social Problem Solving

This module will instruct children to think of alternative responses
when confronted with interpersonal conflict. They will also learn to consider the consequences of these responses and be given opportunities to
practice considering and choosing constructive alternatives. Individualized
goals that might be addressed include (1) increasing the frequency of
constructive alternatives considered when confronted with conflict; (2)
decreasing the frequency of aggressive, impulsive responses in conflict
situations; and (3) improving peer relationships.

ORGANIZATION OF SOCIAL GROWTH MODULES

The organization of these Social Growth Modules was adapted from the format used in the Social Skills Training Modules developed by Michelson, Sugai, Wood and Kazdin (1983). The organization is similar in its inclusion of a rationale for group leaders; a verbal presentation of the module topic for children; and the use of modeling, rehearsal, and feedback. Both sets of modules also close with a group discussion and a review of homework assignments. The Social Skills Training Modules have a strong empirical basis and are well grounded theoretically within a social learning framework. These characteristics provided an excellent foundation for the development of the Social Growth Program, which emphasizes social learning, developmental, and individual differences perspectives.

One of the primary differences between our Social Growth Modules and the Social Skills Training Modules is the population of children targeted for services. The Social Growth Modules are geared toward young elementary school children 5 to 9 years old, whereas the Social Skills Training Modules are geared toward somewhat older children, 8 to 12 years old. Thus, the Social Growth Program places a greater emphasis on basic skills such as active listening and does not include modules more relevant for older children (e.g., heterosexual social skills). In a similar vein, the Social Growth Program introduces children to module topics in a way that reflects the cognitive level and attentional capacity of younger children.

Other differences between these programs are apparent in the Social Growth Program's emphasis on individual differences and developmental perspectives. The Social Growth Program emphasizes setting individualized goals for each participant and choosing modules in keeping with these goals. It also takes a strong developmental approach in its presentation of module preparation ideas for kindergarten–second-grade and second-grade–fourth-grade children.

IMPLEMENTATION OF SOCIAL GROWTH PROGRAM

Implementation of the Social Growth Program can be a fun, challenging, and rewarding experience for the therapist or group leader. Preparation, an ability to build positive, accepting relationships with children, and flexibility are the keys to a successful program.

Designing an Individualized Treatment Program

This initial planning phase requires a thorough individualized assessment (see Chapter 5), the identification of goals, and the choice of appropriate Social Growth Modules. It is a good idea to begin with an overall plan, although flexibility is probably the hallmark of a successful intervention program. It might be useful to rank-order the goal statements that result from the individualized assessment and identify the modules that most clearly relate to these goals. Depending on the goals, a module may be the focus of one, two, three, or even four sessions. A clear discussion with the parents and, possibly, teacher(s) should focus on the nature of these goals. This will enable the mental health professional to establish an informal agreement with them on the approximate number of sessions and begin an ongoing communication about progress toward goals.

Preparing for Program Sessions

An in-depth description of each module with instructional material and preparation ideas for group and individual sessions is presented in Chapter 6. It is helpful to review this material carefully before a session. Each module is organized in the following format:

- Goals
- Rationale
- Preparation Ideas
- Introduction: Instruction/Discussion of New Concepts
- Modeling
- Practice and Constructive Feedback
- Discussion

The session begins with instruction and discussion of new social skills concepts or knowledge. This is followed by modeling provided by the therapist or group leader. Children are then given the opportunity to practice new skills and are offered constructive feedback. In the final phase of the session, the new concepts and practice efforts are discussed.

Setting Up the Room

The physical environment of the room must be conducive to building a positive relationship with the child or children. Is it chaotic and overwhelming, or is it characterized by some sense of structure and organization? Are there areas for quiet thought as well as for active play? Does the room have a warm feeling? Are some things located within the reach and at the eye level of the child? The layout is particularly important if you are working with groups of children. We have found that it's useful to divide one large room (e.g., classroom size) into smaller group discussion, gross motor, family living, arts and crafts, and time-out areas (Kirschenbaum et al., 1976). Figure 1 presents the recommended floor plan originally used in the Social Skills Development Program, one of the forerunners to the

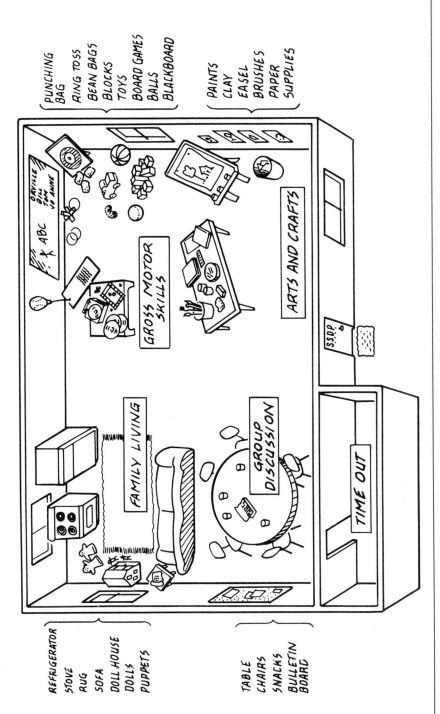

Figure 1   Social Skills Development Program's Playroom (Group Therapy Room) (*From* Kirschenbaum, D. S., et al. (1983). A social competence model meets an early intervention program. *In* D. F. Ricks and B. S. Dohrenwend (Eds.) *Origins of Psychopathology.* New York: Cambridge University Press.)

Labels on the figure:

PUNCHING BAG
RING TOSS
BEAN BAGS
BLOCKS
TOYS
BOARD GAMES
BALLS
BLACKBOARD

PAINTS
CLAY
EASEL
BRUSHES
PAPER
SUPPLIES

GROSS MOTOR SKILLS

ARTS AND CRAFTS

FAMILY LIVING

GROUP DISCUSSION

TIME OUT

S.S.D.P.

REFRIGERATOR
STOVE
RUG
SOFA
DOLL HOUSE
DOLLS
PUPPETS

TABLE
CHAIRS
SNACKS
BULLETIN BOARD

Social Growth Program (Kirschenbaum et al., 1983). This floor plan was also used in the Wisconsin Early Intervention Program (King & Kirschenbaum, 1990). The room divisions minimize confusion and offer some predictability to children (e.g., it's clear where group discussion is held). A therapist working with individual children may well be using a smaller office, and in this case it's important to have a comfortable place with some play materials (e.g., puppets, dollhouse) that will facilitate discussion and the practice of new responses.

Reviewing Goals and Preparing Resource Materials

During the planning time, therapists and group leaders should consider their feelings and reactions to the previous session and, if working with a co-leader, discuss them with that person. Tentative plans can be made about the module that will be the focus of the next session, the individualized goals that will be addressed, and the specific techniques that will be used. It helps to practice modeling or role-playing the pertinent skills (e.g., active listening, asking questions) before the session.

Preparation varies for each module. The recommended first module, Who Am I?, is enhanced if name tag materials are available for group sessions and magazines, scissors, and paste are available for individual or group sessions. These supplies can then be used for the "How We're Unique" activity described in Chapter 6. Ditto sheets titled "All About Me" or "I Can" might also be used with third- or fourth-grade children. In contrast, puppets are useful in presenting the module called Self-Control to younger children, supplies for recording or graphing progress in presenting it to older children.

Each module also includes recommendations for two types of take-home materials that are included in an effort to increase the generalization of new concepts and skills to other settings. One is a homework assignment, entitled FOR ME, that can be tentatively planned before the session, although changes may need to be made depending on progress during the session. The second is the FOR MY PARENTS AND TEACHERS (group sessions) or FOR MY PARENTS (individual sessions) papers that briefly describe the concepts discussed and practiced during the session, with ideas for how these concepts might be further encouraged in the home or school setting.

Conducting Sessions: General Guidelines

Whether you are conducting individual or group sessions, building a therapeutic relationship with each child is essential. Although this will not be as easy with some children as with others, your efforts to create a safe, predictable environment and to convey a sense of acceptance to each child will be helpful. Once a therapeutic relationship has been established, many children will enter a phase in which they show clear signs of therapeutic progress or social growth during a session. The therapist or group leader then faces the challenge of helping children carry these gains to other settings such as the school and neighborhood.

Building Therapeutic Relationships with Children

The success of the Social Growth Program is somewhat dependent on the relationship the therapist or group leaders have with each child. The introductory meeting with the child should be simple, direct, and sincere. It's important to convey warmth and a sense of acceptance.

Some children may express their individuality right at the start and fail to meet expectations of what "happens next." A helpful attitude is to expect the unexpected and remember that a programmed introduction is likely to fail. Therapists and group leaders should make an effort to remain calm and evaluate their own responses (e.g., anger, anxiety) so that they can deal with these responses in a way that does not interfere with the child's progress. Efforts to "force" children to cooperate may not further the goal of beginning a positive, warm relationship.

In developing a therapeutic relationship with a child, it is important to remember that talking is only one medium and that play is sometimes more comfortable for children. Group leaders and therapists should avoid highly charged questions and challenges until later in the relationship, when rapport has been clearly established. It helps to begin with topics or activities that are generally appropriate with children of that age (e.g., favorite TV shows, video or computer games, neighborhood friends). Confidentiality is an issue that should be dealt with at the beginning. Most children have no familiarity with the extent and limits to confidentiality in therapeutic relationships. It helps to establish some clear guidelines and share them with the child as well as with parents and teachers.

The process of developing a therapeutic relationship is easiest if some structure is provided. This usually involves a discussion of the role of the therapist or group leader, the duration of the relationship, the time limit of sessions, and the location of sessions. In the Social Growth Program, additional structure is offered by the consistent format of the sessions. Regardless of module or social skills concept, sessions will consist of instruction and discussion, modeling, practice, and feedback. Limits are also important in providing structure and assuring each child that he or she will be safe. It's helpful to state limits in positive ways and explain, in simple terms, the reasons for the limits. It sometimes works to have the individual child or group help determine the limits, but the therapist or group leader must consider his or her own tolerance level, for consistency will be important. Common limits include length of the session, respect for individuals (no physical aggression), degree of motor activity allowed (running?), noise level (screaming?), and session requirements (e.g., discussion period at table).

Therapeutic relationships generally progress through predictable phases, and an understanding of these phases may help the therapist maintain an appropriate focus in the face of troubling or confusing behaviors. Children may be anxious, confused, or hyperactive during the "getting to know you phase," but they are usually at least reasonably well behaved. This phase has sometimes been called the "Honeymoon" period, and its length will vary with different children.

The second phase is characterized by some resistance and testing of limits, in whatever way may be characteristic of an individual child. This could involve being late, physically harming others, running around the room, wanting to prolong certain activities, or telling fantastic stories. The therapist should remain calm, ignore negative behaviors and reinforce positive ones when possible, maintain consistent limits, and "wait it out." It's also helpful to talk with the child about his or her feelings and about alternative, more adaptive behaviors. This phase can be emotionally draining for the therapist, who may find that he is becoming very angry with the child or very upset with his lack of progress with the child. It will be important for the therapist to be aware of his anger or disappointment. Sharing feelings and experiences with other therapists or a supervisor can be a useful outlet for these feelings.

Finally, it's always helpful to keep in mind that the difficult phase is often followed by a phase characterized by a strong therapeutic relationship and active therapeutic progress. During this more active working phase, the child may actively take hold of the therapist's or group's values, show clear signs of modeling and imitation of the therapist's or group's behaviors, and work with the therapist to reach individualized goals. This is certainly the most rewarding phase for the therapist.

Enhancing Generalization of Knowledge and Skills

There is ample evidence from many related intervention programs that children do improve their social skills during individual or group sessions (e.g., Ladd, 1981; Michelson et al., 1983; Oden & Asher, 1977). Perhaps the most difficult task of the therapist is to take on the extra work necessary to help the child generalize the new ideas and skills to other settings such as the playground, the living room, and the classroom. The Social Growth Program has some built-in components to assist in this process. The first is the active collaboration with parents and teachers that begins at the time of screening or referral. This is essential to the quality of the individualized assessment as well as to the child's permission to take part and remain in the program. Of equal importance, however, parents' and teachers' understanding of the program will enable them to help children make use of new knowledge and skills in other settings.

The FOR ME (homework assignment) and FOR MY PARENTS AND TEACHERS or FOR MY PARENTS papers that accompany each module are designed to assist in this generalization process. The homework task is not time consuming but does give children an opportunity to work on the new concept or skill in another setting at another time. The papers for parents and teachers offer an opportunity for children to share information about skills they are learning and working on during sessions. If an active collaboration has been developed with the parent or teacher, these papers may be discussed in the home or classroom and the ideas for promoting the generalization of skills may be put into practice. The more significant others, such as parents and teachers, emphasize and reinforce new skills, the more likely it is that a child will value their importance and work to improve them. Once a child begins to use these skills in natural contexts (e.g., on the playground), the skills are often naturally reinforced as other children respond in positive ways.

Special Issues for Implementation with Groups of Children

Given that the Social Growth Program has been designed to help young children develop social skills or effective ways of relating to others, it is ideally suited for implementation with groups of children. Within a group setting, children are offered many opportunities to understand themselves in relation to others, to practice new ways of relating to others, and to overcome social fears. The challenges for the mental health professional include establishing a group that will maximize the likelihood of program effectiveness for individual children and determining the frequency of and total number of group sessions feasible in the treatment setting. Finally, the selection, training, and supervision of group leaders is generally coordinated by the mental health professional responsible for program development.

Group Size and Composition

We recommend implementation with small groups of four to six children. This small group size has several advantages. It is possible to create a relatively "safe," nonthreatening setting where children can try out new behaviors and ways of responding to other children and participate in group discussions. This is crucial for success in working with shy or anxious children as well as aggressive children who have earned a reputation of "bully." In larger groups of children, such as in a classroom or on a playground, shy children are likely to withdraw from trying out new behaviors and aggressive children are likely to live up to their "bully" reputation. A second advantage of a small group is the greater proportion of time available for each child to practice and obtain individualized, constructive feedback. Children will benefit from close guidance while they are practicing new skills.

Whenever possible, the program coordinator should strive to establish groups of four to six children that are fairly homogeneous in age and developmental level. This will enable group leaders to plan their introductory remarks and role-plays in keeping with interpersonal themes or topics appropriate for the entire group. Although expectancies will always need to vary somewhat for individual children in the group, wide differences in expectancies may interfere with the development of a cohesive working group.

Depending on the number of children referred, it may be possible to assign children to groups according to their individualized goals, thereby enabling the program coordinator to design a program (series of modules) that closely matches the needs of each child in the group. Despite the attractiveness of this possibility, we have found that most children can derive some benefit from each of the modules. Also, a group composed of children who begin with varying skills can be helpful during the practice phase of group sessions. Some children may be able to model assertive skills for other children but may have a great deal of difficulty with active listening. Other children may do well in self-monitoring and self-control but may be at a loss in resolving social conflicts. As an added bonus, a mixture of social strengths and weaknesses within one group can also help children learn to respect the individual differences and ways in which each group member is unique.

One aspect of child development, readily apparent on any elementary school playground, is that young elementary school children tend to develop same-sex friendships—that is, given a choice during lunch, recess, or classroom free time, girls often choose to sit or play with other girls and boys often choose to spend the time with boys. Although elementary school children's best friends or closest friends tend to be chosen along gender lines, all children must necessarily relate with boys and girls daily in nonchoice activities like reading or arithmetic groups, gym class, and lunch lines. Thus, positive peer relationships during elementary school require that children have the social skills needed to relate effectively with all peers. The Social Growth Program is most appropriately designed with groups composed of boys as well as girls. Group leaders may find that children sometimes pair off in same-sex pairs for role-plays and that the types of examples generated during brainstorming activities differ for boys and girls. For these reasons, it is recommended that a minimum of two girls or two boys be included in each group.

Program Length and Group Session Frequency

The Social Growth Program can vary in length according to the priorities and scheduling constraints within the school or clinic setting. The Wisconsin Early Intervention Program, on which this program is largely based, consisted of twice-weekly sessions across a 12-week program period (King and Kirschenbaum, 1990) and included all nine modules now presented in the Social Growth Program. Depending on time constraints and the individual needs of the children referred, once-weekly or twice-weekly sessions can be arranged for a varying number of weeks. Although we have not researched the effectiveness of programs of varying lengths, we would recommend a minimum of eight group sessions. This number of sessions enables the group to develop some level of comfort and cohesion within which to begin learning and practicing new social skills.

Selecting Group Leaders

Group sessions are most effectively facilitated by two group leaders. These group leaders can model social skills such as active listening, empathy, and social problem solving and can complete role-plays with each other. One of the leaders can also be available to work with individual children in the group who may need special coaching or help with some of the module activities. Finally, a second group leader is no longer a luxury when behavioral management problems arise during group sessions. Despite efforts to develop a positive group culture with clear and consistent limit setting, some behavioral problems will need to be addressed on an individual basis. One group leader can continue the group session while the other handles an individual behavioral difficulty.

The Use of Paraprofessional Group Leaders.   Most schools will not have the luxury of staffing each group with two trained professionals. Whenever possible, we recommend that one professional pair up with one paraprofessional to co-lead group sessions. With adequate training and supervision, however, it is also possible to have group sessions co-led by two paraprofessionals. Paraprofessionals can expand the reach of a program geometrically while considerably reducing its cost.

The importance of paraprofessionals within the helping services fields can hardly be overestimated. Paraprofessionals comprise the largest category of mental health staff—with an estimated 150,000 paid paraprofessionals in facilities throughout this country, including more than 10,000 community mental health centers (Durlak, 1983). Thus, this population of helpers represents between 25 and 50 percent of the full-time equivalent staff members in agencies. This impact has certainly been felt in early intervention programs (Cowen et al., 1980, 1983). Thus, in the most recent survey of early intervention programs in this country and elsewhere (Cowen et al., 1983), 87 school districts were identified as having early intervention services, in 300 school buildings serving 167,000 pupils, all of which use paraprofessional helpers extensively—the number of which exceeds 1,200.

Fortunately, a great deal of outcome research has established the effectiveness of paraprofessional helpers beyond question. Out of more than 1,000 outcome studies using paraprofessional therapists, no more than 20 have reported negative results (Durlak, 1983). Benefits of using paraprofessionals have emerged for all types of helping roles, treatment programs, target problems, and client populations. In fact, the data generally suggest that within the clinical contexts examined to date, paraprofessionals produce effects that are at least as good as—and, in several well-controlled cases, significantly better than—those obtained by professionals (Durlak, 1979).

Figure 2 presents a job description for a paraprofessional group leader. This job description is a modification of that used to recruit "elderly" paraprofessionals for the Wisconsin Early Intervention Program (King & Kirschenbaum, 1990). The paraprofessional group leader may be a voluntary or paid part-time worker. These persons are extensively screened and selected for their willingness to make a commitment to the entire program (training, group sessions, supervisions) as well as their possession of personal qualities compatible with working closely with young

---

JOB DESCRIPTION
PARAPROFESSIONAL GROUP LEADER

Supervision

The paraprofessional group leader works under the direct, close supervision of the school's mental health professionals.

Duties

The paraprofessional group leader carries out duties aimed at achieving children's individual goals as established by the Social Growth Program coordinator. The paraprofessional group leader will be required to carry out the following specific duties, among others:

a. Attend and participate in extensive orientation and training sessions and weekly supervisory sessions. Share information regarding children's progress and planning with group co-leader.

b. Establish rapport and productive relationships with children, parents, school-based professionals, and other program team members.

c. Co-lead children's Social Growth groups, with consultation and help from school mental health professionals.

d. Keep all information concerning individual children and families strictly confidential.

e. Write process notes and complete form required for the purpose of program evaluation.

Entry Requirements

The paraprofessional group leader is selected on the basis of interpersonal and experiential qualities rather than educational ones. Thus, there are no specific educational requirements. An intensive, 45-hour training program will prepare the paraprofessional group leader for his/her role within the school.

Applicants should have warmth, should enjoy working with children, should be reliable, adaptable, and have the ability to empathize with people. They should feel comfortable in an interpersonal context. Also, since the job can often be demanding physically as well as emotionally, it is important that candidates enjoy reasonably good health and vitality.

The applicant need not pass a written examination for the position. However, careful prescreening of candidates will require personal interviews.

Evaluation

Each paraprofessional group leader will be evaluated at the completion of the first three-month period by the responsible school professional. This evaluation will reflect the paraprofessional group leader's performance in meeting specific program objectives. Each paraprofessional group leader evaluated will have an opportunity to read and discuss the evaluation with the people doing the evaluation.

Contract

Because of the important role the paraprofessional group leader will play in the life of the children and in this project, a written contract will be established for each applicant. If the applicant agrees to the responsibilities of the paraprofessional group leader position, he or she will state the commitment in the form of a signed contract.

Figure 2

children. The selection of these workers will probably be made by supervisory and administrative staff, and recruitment guidelines have been established (Durlak, 1983). It is recommended that applicants complete a standard application form with work history and references and participate in interviews with two staff members. These staff interviewers may make use of the eight rating scales displayed in Figure 3, which have been used to identify paraprofessionals exhibiting the characteristics of interpersonal confidence, warmth, and cooperativeness (Cowen et al., 1975; Sandler, 1972).

Training and Supervising Group Leaders

Training and ongoing supervision enable the group leaders to work comfortably and effectively as members of the treatment program. The training topics may vary depending on the background education and experience of selected group leaders, but some information on child development, forming relationships with children, and managing child behavior problems is probably necessary. Confidentiality is another topic that is likely to be addressed in training as well as in ongoing supervision. An outline of the training program used in the Wisconsin Early Intervention Program is presented in Figure 4.

RATING SCALES
FOR PROSPECTIVE PARAPROFESSIONAL GROUP LEADERS

Name of Applicant _____ Total Score _____

Name of Rater _____ Date _____

Circle the number you think best describes the applicant for each scale

1. *Personal Warmth*

7	6	5	4	3	2	1

Seems very warm   Seems very cold

2. *Working with Children*

7	6	5	4	3	2	1

Not enjoy at all   Enjoys very much

3. *Working with Others*

7	6	5	4	3	2	1

Highly capable of   Not at all cooperative:
cooperative work   highly competitive

4. *Independence*

7	6	5	4	3	2	1

Seems highly   Highly capable of
dependent   independent work

5. *Reliability*

7	6	5	4	3	2	1

Highly responsible and   Irresponsible; not likely
would honor commitments   to honor commitments

6. *Stability*

7	6	5	4	3	2	1

Well adjusted, mature   Poorly adjusted; immature

7. *Orientation to New Knowledge*

7	6	5	4	3	2	1

Seems very open to new   Seems closed-minded; rigid
learnings and experiences   in regard to knowledge

8. *Psychological Mindedness*

7	6	5	4	3	2	1

Oriented to fatalistic   Comprehends interactions
religious, moralistic   of personality, environment,
explanations of behavior   culture

Figure 3

WISCONSIN EARLY INTERVENTION:
PARAPROFESSIONAL TRAINING PROGRAM OUTLINE

Format: Each 3-hour morning session will include the following:

1. Present session goals.
2. Present new concepts/skills (lecture, film, role-plays).
3. Review homework/reading assignment and integrate with new concepts/ skills.
4. Break
5. Discuss new concepts/practice new skills.
6. Present homework/reading assignment.
7. Evaluate session.

Session I: Introduction

1. Initiate understanding of prevention model and importance of paraprofessionals.
2. Become acquainted with each other and with project supervisors.
3. Review format and goals of training program.

Session II: Childhood Development and Adjustment

1. Expand awareness of mental health issues: social definitions of normal/ abnormal behavior and the continuum of adjustment.
2. Learn what is meant by "at-risk" children and learn the key developmental tasks of primary grade children.

Session III: Child Relationship Building

1. Forming relationships with children.
2. Practice communication/interview skills.
   Physical attending,
   Active listening,
   Mirroring/Reflecting,
   "I" statements

Session IV, V: Child Management Skills

1. Learn child management techniques:
   Praise, Ignore, Time-out, Removing Rewards, Compliance, Consistency, Clarity, Praise
2. Practice/role-play child management techniques.

Session VI: Children's Social Skills Groups: Introduction

1. Review format and goals.
2. Learn content of modules.
3. Observe role-play presentation of module.

Session VII thru *Session X*: *Children's Social Skills Groups*: *Practice*

1. Practice/Role-play presentation of group lesson modules.
2. Learn to integrate modules into a session with preliminary discussion and freeplay.
3. Discuss group limit-setting and group transition skills.

   —Who Am I?
   —Who Are We? What Are Social Skills?
   —Active Listening
   —Warm Messages
   —Asking Questions
   —Sharing Feelings/Empathy
   —Standing Up for Me
   —Self-Control
   —Social Problem-solving

Session XI: *Confidentiality*

1. General meaning
2. Specific aspects

   —Client identity
   —Evaluation findings
   —Specialist-child, Specialist-parent, Specialist-teacher relationship
   —Session content

3. School staff and confidentiality

   —Principal
   —Teachers
   —Peer specialists
   —Supervisors

Session XII: *School Entry and Collaboration*

1. Increase knowledge of school system and school staff.
2. Learn importance of collaboration with school staff.
3. Review specific nature and importance of close supervision. SEEK HELP WHEN NEEDED.

Session XIII: *Special Issues*

1. Expand awareness of child abuse/neglect.
2. Learn limits/extent of child aide responsibility.
3. Expand awareness of sexual/cultural stereotypes.

Session XIV: *Schedule Coordination*

1. Review specific nature and importance of *required* project forms/progress notes.
2. Develop school teams and set up school time schedule.
3. Meet school principals and available school staff.
4. Evaluate training program.

Figure 4

Ongoing supervision generally consists of a minimum of one hour per week in addition to the one-hour preparation and review meeting for co-leaders. Besides being supportive, this supervision time enables the group leaders to obtain help with procedural and behavioral management difficulties as well as to evaluate their own responses to individual children.

SUMMARY

The Social Growth Program can be used with an individual child or small groups of children to address social and emotional adjustment problems. The program provides structured, skills-oriented interventions within the context of warm, supportive relationships. The nine Social Growth Program modules can be flexibly integrated into an individualized intervention program. Modules cover skills such as active listening, standing up for oneself, asking questions, and maintaining self-control. The interventions consist of instruction in social skills concepts, discussion, modeling, practice, and feedback. Two of the most challenging and rewarding tasks facing the therapist in this program are building strong relationships with children and working to assure the generalization of new knowledge and skills to natural settings.

5

ASSESSMENT OF YOUNG CHILDREN'S SOCIAL ADJUSTMENT

Our approach to the assessment of young children's social adjustment emphasizes the importance of gathering information that will be helpful in establishing individualized, developmentally appropriate social growth goals. The overall aim is to gather information that will enable you to plan and implement an effective, social competency–oriented intervention program for groups of children within a school system or an individual child or small group of children in your private practice.

Children in elementary school are faced with the dual demands or developmental tasks of developing cooperative, positive peer relationships and learning and achieving academically. Because they are developing at differing rates, have differing temperamental styles, and enter school with differing life experiences, it is inevitable that the very social nature of the school environment will pose difficulties for some children. And, in fact, social and learning problems sometimes first become apparent during the early elementary school years.

The intervention process begins with either a schoolwide screening of children or the referral of an individual child or children. A school system with a proactive approach to the identification and treatment of adjustment problems might conduct a general screening of children after the first one or two months of school and provide appropriate early intervention services. Other schools may have counseling resources that are only available to respond to crises, serious emotional or behavioral problems, or select individual requests for services. In these schools, teachers may refer one or two individual children for counseling services. Depending on the type and availability of these services, teachers or school counselors may also encourage parents to seek help from private, community-based practitioners.

How does the school-based or private, community-based practitioner complete an assessment of social adjustment problems? Following a standard intake interview format, an intensive, individualized assessment can be conducted to identify social situations problematic for the child as well as the nature of the child's difficulties in these situations. This assessment allows the mental health professional to formulate specific behavioral goals. A similar system, used by the PMHP (Cowen, Pederson, Babigian, Izzo, & Trost, 1973), and the SSDP (Kirschenbaum et al., 1983), has been recommended by theoreticians (Dodge, McClaskey, & Feldman, 1985).

Assessment of social adjustment includes the individual child, the social context or setting (including other people in the setting), and the interaction between individual child and setting. We begin by identifying or targeting the problems observed or reported by informants and the social contexts or situations within which these problems occur. Are they cross-situational or situation specific? After the situation-specific social problems have been targeted, it is important to specify components of these problems so that we can design an effective intervention plan.

SCREENING

We include here information on general screening to identify young children at risk for professionals who are involved in or are considering starting up a school-based early intervention program. Screening should be conducted in a positive, collaborative way. The idea is to help referral sources ask, "Which children might most benefit from services aimed at promoting social-cognitive growth and development?" rather than asking, "Which children are mentally ill or behaviorally disordered?" The latter message begins a process of negative labeling and negative expectancies and would (should!) raise anxieties among parents of referred children. Because diverse services are available in many elementary schools, priorities must be set for each child. The goal of the screening phase is to gather information from teachers and parents and make recommendations about which children might most benefit from an early intervention program aimed at promoting social growth.

The screening phase involves: (1) orientation sessions, (2) referral interviews, and (3) teacher-completed referral rating scales. This phase can be expected to identify 15 percent to 25 percent of primary-grade children, although methods can be varied if resources are insufficient to intervene with this many children. Two of the major early intervention programs described in Chapter 3, the PMHP (Cowen et al., 1973) and the SSDP (Kirschenbaum et al., 1983), have intervened with this proportion of primary grade children. The Social Growth Program was piloted with approximately 40 percent of primary-grade children from two schools (King &

Kirschenbaum, 1990). This higher proportion resulted from the high level of demand that promotion of an educational, competency-oriented program created.

Orientation Sessions

General orientation sessions are made available to staff members and parents in participating schools. In an effort to maximize attendance, these sessions might be arranged during regularly scheduled staff and parent-teacher organization (PTO) meetings. During these sessions, the early intervention program director or coordinator should have the opportunity to describe the goal of the program and its focus on promoting social competency. Examples might also be given on the kinds of behaviors that may indicate an early adjustment problem. It is helpful to describe, and perhaps illustrate, a continuum of social competency. Most children's overall level of social competency falls somewhere between the extreme of a popular, sociable, assertive child and a rejected, isolated, and/or aggressive child. The level of competency is influenced by children's temperamental styles; personal preferences, values, and aptitudes; history of interpersonal experiences; and current social skills. It is important to emphasize that the program is not aimed at mass-producing socially competent lookalikes but rather involves individualized goals and respects each child's uniqueness. Following this orientation, the program representative can continue with either or both of two referral methods, screening interviews and teacher-completed rating scales.

Referral Interviews

The program coordinator may choose to interview each primary grade teacher using the Teacher Interview Form developed by Kirschenbaum et al. (1983). Although this screening method is time consuming, it is highly beneficial because it enables the coordinator to build a personal relationship with the referring teacher. The coordinator then reviews the continuum of social competence as indicated on the Teacher Interview Form (Figure 5).

This review includes a discussion of the characteristics of highly competent children as well as less competent children. The interviewer then assists the primary grade teacher in a review of his or her class roster. The teacher is asked to identify classroom children who could be described as highly socially competent and another group of children who have significant problems or deficits in this area. As a conversation ensues about the differences between these two groups of children, it should become apparent that, just as some children benefit from extra help with reading or math skills, other children may benefit from extra help with social skills.

TEACHER INTERVIEW FORM

Teacher's Name ————————————— Interviewer ————

Room number ————————————— Date —————

School —————————————————

1. *Characteristics of Highly Competent Children*
   good student, gutsy (assertive), friendly, follows rules, tolerates frustration.
2. *Characteristics of Less Competent Children*
   acts out (is disruptive, restless), appears moody-withdrawn (immature,
   friendless, unhappy), has difficulty learning (doesn't complete work, trouble following directions).
3. Rank-order identified children below under both low- and high-
   competence categories. Try to identify several children for each category.
   Also, write a brief description of the child's behavior.

High Competence

Child's Name   Brief Description

Most Competent = 1

1. ————————————————————————

2. ————————————————————————

3. ————————————————————————

4. ————————————————————————

5. ————————————————————————

6. ————————————————————————

7. ————————————————————————

8. ————————————————————————

9. ————————————————————————

10. ———————————————————————

Low Competence

Child's Name   Brief Description

Least Competent = 1

1. _____

2. _____

3. _____

4. _____

5. _____

6. _____

7. _____

8. _____

9. _____

10. _____

Figure 5 (*From*: Kirschenbaum, D. S., et al. (1983). A social competence model meets an early intervention program. *In* D. F. Ricks and B. S. Dohrenwend (Eds.) *Origins of Psychopathology.* New York: Cambridge University Press.)

Referral Rating Forms

A second screening method that requires less staff time involves the use of short referral rating forms. A recommended form is the AML School Adjustment Rating Scale (A = Acting-Out, M = Moody-Withdrawn, L = Learning), which was developed by Cowen et al. (1973) and has been used in the PMHP program, the SSDP program, and the piloted Social Growth Program. These forms require teachers to rate frequencies of problem behaviors for each child in their classroom. Teachers can complete these brief forms on all classroom children within approximately 30 minutes. From these forms it is possible to identify children with problems in any of three areas: acting out/aggressive, moody/withdrawn, and learning problems.

Regardless of the method chosen, it will be important to speak with the child's parents, respond to their questions and concerns, and obtain their consent for the child's participation in the program. A more individualized assessment should also be completed before a definite commitment is made regarding program involvement.

INDIVIDUAL ASSESSMENT

The individualized assessment involves multiple strategies including intensive interviews, behavioral rating scales, and observations. The purposes of the assessment are to specify the situation-specific problems, validate those problems by observing the child or interviewing a second informant, and identify contributing factors that could be a focus of intervention.

Interviews

Individual interviews with teachers, parents, and referred children will most likely be the starting point and provide the foundation for your entire assessment. The advantages of the interview have been clearly outlined elsewhere (e.g., Nuttall & Ivey, 1986). For our purposes, however, it is worthwhile to note that the interview offers a personal, flexible approach to gathering useful information. An interview enables the mental health professional to establish some rapport with parents, teachers, and children while gathering historical data, assessing perceptions of the problem, observing interpersonal behaviors, and beginning a functional analysis of the presenting problem. As an assessment tool specifically aimed at identifying individualized social skill goals, the following three-step interview process is recommended:

Establishing Rapport and Building Trust

The initial phase involves building a working alliance with the interviewee. This task is facilitated by a professional, friendly, warm, and caring attitude characterized by active listening and respect for the interviewee. A description of the structure and purpose of the interview is helpful in building rapport and setting the parent, teacher, or child at ease.

Gathering General Information

In this phase of the interview, interviewees are questioned about their perceptions of the child's strengths as well as social adjustment problems and the interviewee's previous efforts to address problems. Parents are also asked questions about the child's developmental, school, family, and medical history. The scope of the child's problems and the appropriateness of an early intervention program such as the Social Growth Program are considered. Some children will be referred for early intervention services who actually have severe or multiple problems that cannot be addressed by such services. These children will need to be referred for the appropriate evaluations (e.g., physical exam, psychiatric and/or psychological evaluations, vision or hearing exams) and services. If the referred child is already obtaining mental health services from a psychiatrist, psychologist, social worker, or counselor outside the school system, it is extremely important to gather this information and permission to conduct a telephone interview with the service provider. This interview is necessary to determine whether or not the child would benefit from the additional services of this program.

Gathering Specific Information: Behavioral Interview

Each interview can then proceed with a functional analysis of presenting problems. It is useful to begin by identifying the specific social contexts or settings that are problematic for the child. How does the child behave at home versus school? How does the child behave during structured and unstructured classroom activities? on the playground? After determining whether or not the problems are cross-situational or situation specific, the professional's task is to identify contributing factors that could be a focus of intervention.

Let's review the components of socially competent behavior as a useful guide for this portion of the interview:

- *Knowledge of Appropriate Social Behavior*

Is the problem caused by a lack of knowledge or social understanding? What knowledge is required for effective responses in this situation? Children reveal knowledge deficits when they say, "I don't know how to ask for help when I'm confused," or "I don't know when it's okay to tell on Johnny."

- *Performance of Age-Appropriate Social Behavior*

Perhaps the child knows or understands social rules and appropriate social responses and the problem reflects a deficit in behavioral skills. Is the performance problem caused by a lack of self-control skills ("I *know* what I should have done, but I was so angry I just lost it") or communication skills ("I don't know how to call Sam back on the phone")? Is the performance problem caused by social anxieties or inhibition ("I'm afraid to ask a question and I just keep getting more and more confused and upset")? Is it a problem of motivation ("The only way I get any help is by screaming!")? What are the antecedents and consequences of socially appropriate and inappropriate (skilled and unskilled) behaviors in these situations? (What is commonly going on just before the problem occurs or the child misbehaves? What do other children usually do in response to this behavior? What do you usually do?)

- *Self-Monitoring*

By the start of elementary school, most children have some awareness of the effects of their behaviors on others. Children vary a great deal in the extent to which they monitor their own behaviors, but some degree of monitoring can usefully guide their interactions and contribute to positive social growth. Some children referred for services may self-monitor to such an extent that they "freeze" and are anxious and withdrawn, lacking in spontaneity. More frequently, children are referred because of impulsive, acting-out, unmonitored behavioral responses. These children fail to take note of interpersonal cues and evaluate their own behaviors and how these affect others.

The interviewer can use information from this interview to generate ideas about appropriate interventions and individualized goals. These ideas can be further investigated and assessed by gathering additional rating scale and observational data.

Behavioral Rating Scales

Behavioral rating scales completed by teachers and/or parents are useful in identifying the pattern of a child's strengths and weaknesses in the school or home setting. It is not prudent, however, to use these ratings as the sole assessment instrument; individual raters may respond in a biased manner, and these scales provide descriptive, but not causal, information about the reasons for the child's problem behaviors. These scales usually list many specific behaviors or characteristics, and the rater's task is to indicate those that apply to the child.

There are many scales of deviant or problem behaviors and few that assess children's strengths or competencies. One noteworthy instrument, however, is the *Health Resources Inventory* (HRI; Gesten, 1976). This 54-item, five-point Likert-type scale yields scores on five factors or dimensions: Good Student, Gutsy, Peer Sociability, Rule Following, and Frustration Tolerance. It also yields an overall Competency summary score. A companion, problem-focused scale is the *Classroom Activity Rating Scale* (CARS; Lorion, Cowen, & Caldwell, 1975). The CARS consists of 41 items that are also rated on five-point Likert-type scales. These items describe problem behaviors and yield scores on three factors: Acting-Out, Moody-Withdrawn, and Learning Difficulty. It is also possible to compute an overall Maladjustment score from the CARS.

If time constraints prohibit the use of these two scales, another possibility is a scale that was developed from the HRI and CARS, the *Teacher-Child Rating Scale* (T-CRS; Hightower, Work, Cowen, Lotcyzewski, Spinell, Guare, & Rohrbeck, 1986). This 42-item, five-point Likert-type scale can be used to assess teacher perceptions of children's behavioral problems and competencies. Representative items include the following: "Joins peer group activities," "Accepts things not going his/her way," "Constantly seeks attention," and "Accepts imposed limits." The T-CRS yields scores on six factors: Acting-Out, Shy-Anxious, Learning Skills, Frustration Tolerance, Assertive Social Skills, and Task Orientation.

Self-report rating scales have also been developed to assess children's specific social skills. Although these may be of little use with young primary-grade children because of reading levels, they may help in the assessment of third- and fourth-grade children. The *Children's Assertive Behavior Scale* (CABS) requires the child or other informant, such as a parent or teacher, to rate the child's social skills (Michelson & Wood, 1980; Michelson et al., 1983). The scale's 27 items describe a range of social situations (e.g., making complaints or requests, beginning conversations) and possible responses that vary in degree of passivity and aggression. The child or other informant is asked to choose the response that best reflects the child's response tendencies.

The Matson Evaluation of Social Skills with Youngsters (MESSY) was developed with 62-item self-report and 64-item teacher report forms that assess a wide range of social behaviors (Matson, Rotatori, & Helsel, 1983). These forms also use five-point Likert-type scales. The teacher report form results in two factors, Inappropriate Assertiveness/Impulsivity and Appropriate Social Skills. The self-report form yields two similar factors as well as three additional factors: Impulsive/Recalcitrant, Overconfident, and Jealousy/Withdrawal.

Observations

Observational assessment is both extremely valuable and labor intensive. It can be completed with the help of a structured coding system or can consist of a simple, narrative recording. The Social Competence Classroom Behavioral Observation System (SCCBOS) is an 11-category observational system developed by one of the present authors in conjunction with his colleagues (Kirschenbaum, Steffen, & D'Orta, 1978). The SCCBOS is easier to use than many more detailed systems and has the added advantage of assessing positive, adaptive behaviors as well as areas of difficulty. Figure 6 includes a description of the 11 categories assessed by the SCCBOS. The SCCBOS was specifically designed to assess task irrelevant, task relevant, and prosocial behaviors within the classroom. Observations can be made in the classroom of a referring teacher. An example of a coding form is presented in Figure 7. This form can be used for recording behaviors that occur in 10-second intervals across a 10-minute observational period.

A second possibility, the Social Skills Development Program (SSDP) Observation Form, was also developed by Kirschenbaum and his colleagues (Kirschenbaum et al., 1983). This form is similar to the SCCBOS in its assessment of children's social competencies as well as weaknesses. It differs from the SCCBOS, however, in two important ways. First, the SSDP Observation Form is more comprehensive in its assessment of children's functioning. Instead of interval counts of specific behaviors, the SSDP Observation Form allows for more qualitative ratings of appearance and mood as well as behaviors (Figure 8).

THE SOCIAL COMPETENCE CLASSROOM
BEHAVIORAL OBSERVATION SYSTEM (SCCBOS)

I. Task-Irrelevant Behaviors

A. Directed Toward Others

1. *Physical Agression (PA)*: Vigorous physical activity directed toward another child (children) or teacher; must involve physical contact with another child or object; must be forceful and connote negative affect.

   Includes: hitting, pushing, shoving, pinching, slapping, poking, or using object to strike another child or teacher or their possessions; includes spitting; must be task irrelevant.

   Does not include: vigorous physical activity directed at a child's own possessions; examples: child vigorously kicking the wall or desk or throwing his/her own object (scored GM).

2. *Disturbing Others (DO)*: Nontask-relevant physical or verbal activity directed toward other children or teacher; requires the co-presence of at least one other person.

   Includes: task-irrelevant disturbances of other children like tapping or talking; examples: calling out to child or teacher when not participating; tugging lightly on hair and clothing; making threatening gestures toward another person; sticking tongue out; raising fist as if to hit; cursing another person.

   Does not include: any instances in which the second person (the child or teacher acted upon) clearly reacts in pain; spitting at a second person.

B. Solitary

3. *Gross Motor (GM)*: Solitary and/or noisy vigorous physical activity engaged in by child that is clearly not relevant.

   Includes: nontask-relevant out of seat; vigorous activities; walking, running, etc.; vigorous solitary behaviors: wall kicking, throwing an object, masturbation. All instances of pencil sharpening that occur after the first one within a 10-minute period score as GMs.

   Does not include: any activity clearly associated with another person (e.g., fighting); kneeling on seat; standing on seat.

4. *Inappropriate Quiet Activity (IQ)*: Solitary, silent, and nonvigorous task-irrelevant physical activity. Timed behavior: instances of IQ and multiple instances of IQ must occur during full 20 second observation.

   Includes: task-irrelevant playing with toys and pencils under desk; eating; sleeping; writing on desk; looking around; lightly stroking hair, face, or head; standing; not following teacher directive or not responding to personal teacher question.

Does not include: whispering; body rocking; rocking or balancing chair.

5. *Vocalization (V)*: Solitary verbal or nonverbal task-irrelevant sounds.

Includes: task-irrelevant singing, crying, screaming, or humming; talking to self; whistling; more than three sneezes or coughs within a 10-minute period (except if child has cold).

Does not include: calling out to teacher; any verbal threats or sounds directed toward another person.

II. Task-Relevant Behaviors

  A. Directed Toward Others

    1. *Teacher Cooperation (TC)*: Task-relevant physical or verbal activity directed toward the teacher.

    Includes: task-relevant or appropriate hand raised to ask questions in class; teacher asks kid to pull up shades; doing something the teachers asks for; being a line leader; asking a question about content of lesson.

    Does not include: jumping up at inappropriate time to ask question (would be scored DO); asking teacher for approval.

    2. *Peer Cooperation (PC)*: Task-relevant physical or verbal activity directed toward child (children).

    Includes: task-relevant sharing objects; talking quietly; sharing equipment with other child; group play; being a class helper (e.g., giving out paper); must involve another child; not teacher and not solitary.

    Does not include: pencil sharpening; doing anything the teacher says to do; calling out answers.

  B. Solitary

    3. *Appropriate Solitary Activity (AS)*: Solitary task-relevant physical activity.

    Includes: task-relevant independent attention to seat work; playing by self.

    Does not include: any activity directly involving another child; any teacher-helper activity even if teacher doesn't talk to kid at a particular time (e.g., giving out papers at 10:00 A.M. every day).

III. Prosocial Behaviors

    1. *Affection (A)*: Positive physical expression directed toward or about another child or teacher.

    Includes: hugging, kissing, hand-holding, nonaggressive stroking, giving away a possession.

    Does not include: tapping another child for attention even when task relevant.

2. *Smiling/Laughing (SL)*: Smiling or laughing directed at another person or group activity.

   Includes: any instance of SL during teacher presentations or group discussions; nontask-relevant SL is counted if more than one child is involved.

   Does not include: laughing or smiling by oneself when doing quiet seat work.

3. *Assertion (AT)*: Verbal or nonverbal expression about a personal wish, feeling, or desire.

   Includes: joke telling; appropriate rule questioning; limit setting; expression of feeling statements (e.g., "I'm happy," "I'm sad"); seeking approval from teacher; any "why" questions about process, like "Why should we read the book?"; being a leader and moving kids around; pointing to a seat for a child to go to.

   Does not include: content-related (not process-related) questions like, "Why did Columbus discover America?" "What page should I turn to?"

Figure 6

The SSDP Observation Form may also be more useful if you would like a clear assessment of children's behaviors in multiple settings or in a nonclassroom setting such as the playground or lunchroom. Because of the labor-intensive nature of any observational effort, it is helpful first to gather interview information on the specific social situations or contexts that are problematic for a child. Arrangements can then be made to observe the child in those situations.

If you prefer a more flexible, unstructured approach to observational assessment, you can record a narrative of the behavior of the child and others with whom she interacts in a given setting. This narrative can then be translated in terms of the child's behaviors and antecedents and consequences. Private, community-based practitioners may not have the luxury of observing children within the problematic home and/or school settings. It may be possible, however, to have a teacher or parent record information during a designated time period. A structured and simple recording system would be provided to the teacher or parent. This may consist of a record of instances of verbal aggression and others responses during a given time period (e.g., classroom free play) or an event (frequency) count that represents a tally of occurrences of a targeted problem in a given situation. (Please refer to Bellack and Hersen [1988] for a complete review of behavioral observation techniques in natural settings.)

SOCIAL COMPETENCE CLASSROOM BEHAVIORAL OBSERVATION SYSTEM (SCCBOS)

| Intervals (20 second) | Task Irrelevant | | | | | Task Relevant | | | Prosocial | | |
| | Directed Toward Others | | Solitary | | | Directed Toward Others | | Solitary | | | |
	PA	DO	GM	IQ	V	TC	PC	AS	A	SL	AT
1	X	X	X	X	X	✓	✓	✓	✓	✓	✓
2		✓	✓	X	X	✓	✓	✓	X	✓	✓
3	X	X	X	✓	X		✓	✓	X	✓	✓
4				✓		✓	✓		✓	✓	X
5	✓				X	✓	X	X	✓	✓	Y
6	X	X	X	X		✓	X	✓	✓	✓	✓
7	X	✓	X	X	X	X	✓	✓	✓	✓	✓
8	X	✓	X	X	X	✓	✓	✓			
9		✓	X	X	X	✓	✓	✓	✓	✓	✓
10	✓	X	X	X	X	X	✓	✓	✓	✓	2
11	3	3	1	1	1	7	7	6	9	10	8
12											
13											
14											

15										
16										
17										
18										
19										
20										
21										
22										
23										
24										
25										
26										
27										
28										
29										
30										

PA = Physical Aggression; DO = Disturbing Others; GM = Gross Motor; IQ = Inappropriate Quiet Activity; V = Vocalization;
tion; TC = Teacher Cooperation; PC = Peer Cooperation; AS = Appropriate Solitary Activity; A = Affection; SL = Smiling/
Laughing; AT = Assertion

Figure 7

P.A = 3
D.O = 3

10 second across 10 min

SOCIAL SKILLS DEVELOPMENT PROGRAM
OBSERVATION FORM

Child: _____   Teacher: _____

Grade: _____   Amt. of Time Observed: _____

Date: _____   Observer: _____

I. Classroom Environment

    A. Circle a number

    B. Comments:

Very structured ("tight ship")   Very loose

    1   2   3   4   5   6   7

II. Observation of Child: Rate only those items that apply based on your observations:

    (1 = low frequency/intensity to 3 = high frequency/intensity)

    High Competence   *Low Competence*

    A. Physical Appearance

         _3_ clean   ____ dirty

         _3_ neat   ____ sloppy

         ____ average size (age approx.)   ____ unusually big or small

         _3_ looks healthy   ____ looks sickly

         ____ well coordinated   _3_ poorly coordinated

         _9_ Total   _3_ Total

    Comments (note apparent physical limitations or problems related to physical health):

    B. Seatwork Observation: 10 minutes

         _2_ time on task (2½–5 min. = 1; 5–7½ = 2; 7½+ = 3)   ____ frequent daydreaming or frequent out of seat

         _1_ positive attitude toward task   ____ negative attitude toward task

         _3_ helping, cooperating with peers   _1_ talking, disturbing peers

_____ average activity level ____ excessively active/passive

_____ seems liked _3_ seems disliked

_6_ Total _4_ Total
Comments:

C. Mood-Affect: How does this child seem to feel today?

_____ calm (relaxed) _3_ tense (anxious

_____ warm (affectionate) _3_ hostile (angry)

_____ happy (smiles, laughs) _3_ sad (frown, hangs head)

_____ confident (assertive) _____ insecure ("clingy," scared)

_____ expressive (responsive) _____ flat affect (expressionless)

_____ Total _9_ Total
Comments:

D. Relationship with Teacher

1. Teacher Toward Child

_3_ praised _____ criticized

_3_ chosen for special _____ punished (verbal/phys.)
     task(s)
_____ seems to like child _____ seems to dislike child

_6_ Total _____ Total
Comments:

Teacher could encourage
positive reinforcement.

2. Child Toward Teacher

_____ works independently: approp. help seeking

_____ excessive attention seeking

_____ complies with teacher directions

_3_ passively ignores teacher directions

_____ appropriately eager to cooperate

_3_ actively opposes teacher directions

_____ Total

_4_ Total

Comments:

E. Playground (or Lunchroom) Observation: 10 Minutes

_____ helpful, cooperative with other(s)

_____ hostile aggressive toward other(s)

_____ initiates interaction with other(s)

_3_ excludes self from interaction(s)

_____ approached for interaction(s) by others

_____ excluded by others

_____ participates in organized play

_3_ engages in erratic, confused play activity

_____ seems liked by others

_3_ seems disliked by others

_____ Total

_9_ Total

Comments:

Summary

I.   Classroom Environment:

II. Observations of Child:

	High Competence	Low Competence
A. Physical Appearance	3	___
B. Seatwork	___	3
C. Mood-Affect	___	2
D. Relationship with Teacher	___	2
1. Teacher Toward Child	3	___
2. Child Toward Teacher	___	2
E. Playground		
Total:	6	9

Figure 8

DEVELOPING INDIVIDUALIZED SOCIAL GROWTH GOALS

The formulation of specific social growth goals is only possible after a thorough assessment and a clear conceptualization of a child's difficulties. These goals enable service providers as well as teachers, parents, and children to maintain a clear and shared focus on the purpose of interventions. It also enables the service provider to tailor an intervention program specifically to a child's needs. A record of each child's goals can help keep teachers, parents, and children on track and facilitate communication among these individuals. An Individual Goals Form is displayed in Figure 9.

The following list of goal statements is provided as a guide. Each general goal statement is followed by a number of more specific behavioral goal statements. This guide may be used in designing an individualized Social Growth Program because each goal suggests the appropriate use of one or more modules in the program.

RECORD OF INDIVIDUAL GOALS

Child's Name _____

Staff Member _____

Date _____

Each goal that is circled below is an objective that we are working toward with
_____ in the Social Growth Program. Your suggestions
and support are most welcome.

Goal Statements   *Comments About Progress*

A. To Increase Self-Understanding:

B. To Enhance Positive Self-Image:

C. To Increase Understanding of Others
    and Cooperation with Others:

D. To Increase Understanding of
    Personal Rights and Frequency of
    Assertive, Mastery-Oriented Behaviors:

E. To Improve Self-Control:

F. To Improve Social Problem-Solving Skills:

G. Other:

Additional Comments:

Kirshenbaum, D. S., Klei, R. G., Brown, J. E. III, and DeVoge, J. B. (1979). A
non-experimental, but useful, evaluation of a therapy/consultation early intervention
program. *In* G. Landsberg, W. D. Neigher, R. J. Hammer, C. Windle, and J. R. Woy
(eds.) Evaluation in Practice: A Sourcebook of Program Evaluation Studies from
Mental Health Care Systems in the United States. Rockville, MD: US Department of
Health, Education, and Welfare.

Figure 9

Goal Statements

Module(s)		GOALS
	1.	**To Increase Self-understanding**
1,6	a.	To increase verbalization of likes and dislikes
1	b.	To increase accurate description of physical appearance
1,4,6	c.	To increase accurate description of feelings
1,6,7	d.	To increase recognition and verbalization of own needs
	2.	**To Enhance Positive Self-image**
1,7	a.	To increase frequency of realistic, positive statements about self
1–9	b.	To increase frequency of behaviors that require risk taking in group
1–9	c.	To increase frequency of maintaining positive mood when negative feedback or failure experiences occur
1–9	d.	To increase frequency of self-expression via eye contact, giving and receiving compliments, sharing thoughts and feelings
	3.	**To Increase Understanding of and Cooperation with Others**
2,3,6	a.	To increase accurate description of how others are similar and different from self
2,3,4,6,9	b.	To increase frequency of helping, sharing, cooperative behaviors
3,8	c.	To increase length of time one can listen without talking about self or interrupting
2,3,4,6,9	d.	To increase understanding of how own behaviors affect others
	4.	**To Increase Understanding of Personal Rights and Frequency of Assertive, Mastery-oriented Behaviors**
5,7,9	a.	To increase frequency of verbalized questions when confused or afraid in new situations
5,7,9	b.	To increase understanding of rights to be safe, voice some complaints, and refuse some requests
2,4,6,7,8	c.	To increase constructive expression of dislikes and complaints
	5.	**To Improve Self-control**
8	a.	To increase proportion of on-task behavior
8	b.	To increase length of time engaged in appropriate work or play without external reinforcement
8,9	c.	To decrease frequency of aggressive acting out when provoked
	6.	**To Improve Social Problem-solving Skills**
9	a	To increase accurate recognition of interpersonal conflicts
9	b.	To increase number of constructive alternative solutions to conflict
9	c.	To increase clear verbalization of problem-solving steps
9	d.	To increase clear verbalization of consequences of various alternatives
2,3,4,6,8,9	e.	To increase duration of cooperative play with peers

Case Illustration

Jason is a 5-year-old kindergarten boy referred by his teacher for early intervention services. He is beginning to gain a reputation for aggressive bullying behaviors that include hitting, kicking, and verbal outbursts. The school year started just three weeks ago and Jason's teacher is trying to grasp the individual needs of 20 new kindergarten children. She is aware that another child could be hurt by Jason's aggressive behavior and Jason could face social rejection, continuing self-esteem problems, and an increasingly burdensome negative reputation.

Getting Started

A careful evaluation of Jason's difficulties will require us to enter Jason's world, talk with Jason as well as significant adults in his life, and observe his exchanges with others. We cannot conduct a useful, ecologically sound assessment from a distance and must initiate an active collaborative relationship with Jason's parents and teachers at the time of referral. Making this connection enables the mental health professional to build a positive working relationship with teachers and parents, who are critical to the assessment phase as well as the success of any intervention. Interviews, observations, and parent- and teacher-completed questionnaires will be primary sources of information.

Assessment Data

We begin with an introductory interview with Jason's teacher. It is clearly stated to the teacher that the purpose of this first interview is to make an initial determination on the appropriateness of the Social Growth Program. Enough information is gathered to determine whether or not parents should be contacted for more information as well as whether or not a more complete assessment should be conducted. After listening carefully to the teacher's descriptions of Jason's problem behaviors (verbal and physical aggression toward peers, low frustration tolerance), we ask questions about the situational context for these behaviors. The teacher indicates that Jason's low frustration tolerance is apparent in multiple situations (classroom group assignments, lunchroom waiting lines, playground games) but that the aggression is only directed toward peers. We also learn that the teacher's only previous effort to resolve the problem (school year just started three weeks ago) was to establish and discuss with children a set of clear rules for classroom and playground behaviors. Questions about Jason's strengths reveal that Jason's actual performance on learning tasks is about average and that he has reasonably good verbal skills and can be appropriately assertive at times.

This initial information suggests the probable appropriateness of the Social Growth Program, and, with the teacher's recommendation, we contact Jason's parents for additional information. It usually works best if the child's teacher first notifies the parents of her concern, elicits their interest in working together to address the concern, obtains permission to address the concern formally with Social Growth Program staff, and lets parents know to expect a call from the Social Growth Program. This approach enhances rapport and trust among parents, teacher, and Social Growth Program staff.

The interview with Jason's parents reveals that he has had no previous mental health services and that he was proclaimed a "picture of physical health" at his kindergarten checkup. A brief developmental history indicates that Jason's prenatal and perinatal birth histories are without complications and that he reached developmental milestones (e.g., walking, talking) at age-appropriate times. He has been raised in an intact middle-class family, and began attending preschool at the age of three years. Jason's parents also noted that Jason has been a "more difficult child" than their 6-year-old daughter. They describe him as an "outgoing, action-oriented kid" who's never been afraid to take risks. They also talked about screaming and hitting episodes with his sister and noted that Jason "threw tantrums" when he could not have what he wanted.

Based on teacher and parent interview material, Jason's problems do not seem to reflect a serious mental or physical disorder. A determination is made to continue with a more complete assessment that culminates in the specification of individualized goals and an intervention plan.

A second, brief interview is scheduled with Jason's teacher. This more focused behavioral interview assesses the teacher's view of whether or not Jason has knowledge of behaviors that would be more appropriate when he becomes frustrated or is provoked by peers. Information about his social skills, his awareness of how his behaviors affect others, and the antecedents and consequences of his outbursts is gathered.

The Social Growth Program staffperson requests that the teacher also complete the *Teacher-Child Rating Scale* (T-CRS; Hightower et al., 1986). This scale is chosen because it is relatively easy to complete, it assesses social behavioral strengths and problems, and it has good psychometric properties. Scoring reveals that Jason is neither shy nor anxious, he is usually well oriented to classroom tasks, and he has a low frustration tolerance, with a tendency to "act out."

Because Jason's problems with frustration tolerance and aggressive behavior seem to occur in multiple settings, a decision is made to use the SSDP Observation Form (see Figure 8). This form will guide our observations of Jason's strengths and weaknesses in classroom and playground settings. We also decide to jot down notes about observed antecedents and consequences of Jason's problem behaviors. This information will help us understand more specifically the types of events that are most frustrating for Jason. It will also aid us in our efforts to understand ways in which the environment and persons in it may be encouraging, or at least not discouraging, Jason's problem behaviors.

Integrating Assessment Data and Formulating Case from Developmental, Social Learning, and Individual Differences Perspectives

From a developmental perspective, we're aware that elementary school has presented a new challenge to Jason. Although he has attended preschool the past two years, his preschool group consisted of ten children, he attended on a part-time basis, and much of his time was spent in free choice activities. Now Jason has encountered increasing pressure to adapt to a larger group setting with more structured activities and more demands for cooperative behavior.

As we discussed in Chapter 2, elementary school offers exciting opportunities (and sometimes frustrating challenges) to belong to cooperative peer groups and master academic material. Some children enter kindergarten with the prerequisite skills and adaptive style to manage easily and enjoy the new experience. Other children, such as Jason, are struggling with emerging skills and, perhaps, a less adaptive behavioral style. Jason's problems do not seem to reflect any major developmental delays or mental disorders. They can be addressed in a sensitive way that gives him a boost and avoids negative labeling.

In terms of social learning principles, we discovered during our interviews that Jason can verbalize appropriate behaviors for many situations (upset over class assignment, peer name calling, wishing to join a group of children). He has the knowledge to behave appropriately but has newly emerging skills. Because his skills are not solidly in place, he finds it difficult to display them when he's upset or emotionally aroused. It seems that Jason has "always been" sociable and extroverted. He wants to play with peers much of the time but lacks the skills and confidence to assert himself in an honest way that doesn't infringe upon the rights of other children. Jason's confidence and skill deficits, however, have not inhibited him from seeking out peers. Rather, he has forced himself into peer groups physically or made himself the center of negative attention. This has set up a vicious circle wherein other children provoke Jason and he responds aggressively.

Tentative Intervention Plan

Jason's school has a Social Growth Program that works with children in small groups. Because Jason's difficulties are addressed by several Social Growth Modules, the decision is made to include Jason in a new group that is starting soon. Because of the small size of the group (five children) and the ample time allotted for practice and feedback, it will be possible to address our individualized goals for Jason. The use of Social Growth

Modules will be combined with ongoing feedback and consultation with teachers and parents. This will maximize collaborative efforts to assist Jason as well as the likelihood that the gains Jason makes in the group will generalize to home and other school settings.

We choose the following goal statements to guide our efforts with Jason.

1. To Enhance Positive Self-Image
    a. To increase frequency of realistic, positive statements about self
    b. To increase frequency of maintaining positive mood when negative feedback or failure experiences occur
    c. To increase frequency of self-expression via eye contact, giving and receiving compliments, sharing thoughts and feelings
2. To Increase Understanding of/Cooperation with Others
    a. To increase frequency of helping, sharing, cooperative behaviors
    b. To increase understanding of how one's own behaviors affect others
3. To Improve Self-Control
    a. To decrease frequency of aggressive acting-out when provoked
4. To Improve Social Problem-Solving Skills
    a. To increase duration of cooperative play with peers

Our success with Jason will partially reflect our respect for his developing self-esteem as well as his developing social knowledge and skills. Communicating this respect will require a full awareness as well as active praise and acknowledgement of his personal strengths and emerging skills so that Jason has the confidence to persist and struggle in an area where he is having trouble.

RESEARCH EVALUATION: WISCONSIN EARLY INTERVENTION PROGRAM

Assessment is the cornerstone of effective treatment planning as well as of a meaningful program evaluation. The Wisconsin Early Intervention Program (King & Kirschenbaum, 1990), on which the Social Growth Program is based, was experimentally evaluated using some of the same assessment instruments discussed earlier in this chapter. The program and its evaluation are briefly presented here as an example of evaluation research.

The Wisconsin Early Intervention Program was designed as a short-term program for low-socioeconomic rural children with social adjustment problems. A multicomponent program conceptualized within a social learning framework, it also represented an effort to make positive use of the experiences and skills of "elderly" (over age 55) persons, who worked as paraprofessional group leaders in participating elementary schools.

Participants

Participants in the Wisconsin Early Intervention Program were 135 kindergarten through fourth-grade students at two rural elementary schools. A total of 82 boys and 53 girls participated, and the mean age of participants was approximately 8 years old. Mass screening of children was done in one of two ways: some teachers participated in a screening interview using the Teacher Referral Form described earlier in this chapter; other teachers completed the AML 11-item rating scale on all children in their classrooms. Regardless of screening method, children whom teachers described as being in the upper 20 percent of their classroom in terms of overall problem behaviors were referred for services. In addition, children who were described as being in the upper 25 percent for internalizing problems (e.g., anxiety, withdrawal, depression) or externalizing problems (e.g., hyperactivity, aggression) were referred for services. Both screening methods seemed to work well, but we generally preferred the more personal contact possible with the screening interview and Teacher Referral Form.

Overall, 53 percent of early elementary school children were referred for services, and 73 percent of those referred obtained parental permission and became actively involved in the program. The relatively high percentage of referred children reflects the active effort to promote Wisconsin Early Intervention as a social development program, thereby minimizing any negative stigma.

Program Services

Wisconsin Early Intervention services included professional consultation with parents and teachers as well as social skills groups led by the trained "elderly" paraprofessionals. All program services were offered during the second semester of the children's school year. In keeping with the requirements of an experimental evaluation, participating children were randomly assigned to intervention conditions nested within schools. Table 1 displays how children were assigned to interventions in the two participating schools and also lists the assessment measures, which will be discussed later.

Within one school, 20 boys and 16 girls were assigned to a "Full Service" condition. These children participated in social skills groups, and their parents and teachers were offered case consultation services. Within

Table 1 Wisconsin Early Intervention: Program Design and Assessment Measures

Services	Number of participants	Measures
SCHOOL A		
Full service: Social skills groups/consultation	36	Teacher-Child Rating Scale Child Behavior Checklist Children's Depression Rating Scale–Revised Aide-Child Rating Scale
Partial service: Consultation only	42	Teacher-Child Rating Scale Child Behavior Checklist Children's Depression Rating Scale–Revised
SCHOOL B		
Partial service: Consultation only	24	Teacher-Child Rating Scale Child Behavior Checklist
No service	25	Teacher-Child Rating Scale Child Behavior Checklist

Note: Complete pre- and postassessments are not available for all participants on all measures. Reprinted with permission from *Journal of Community Psychology*, Vol. 18, April 1990, p. 169.

this same school, 24 boys and 18 girls were assigned to a "Partial Service" condition. Children assigned to this condition did not participate in social skills groups, and their parents and teachers were offered consultation services. Within the second school, some children (16 boys, 8 girls) were assigned to the same "Partial Service" condition. Other children within this school were assigned to the "No Services" condition. Although complete pre- and postassessments were also conducted with this latter group, they received no services during the project period.

Children in the "Full Service" and "Partial Service" conditions were eligible for consultation services. These were made available to teachers on a weekly basis and to parents by appointment as well as before and after parent-teacher conferences without appointments. Consultation services included the provision of information about child development, child behavior management, and child problems that warrant a referral for professional assistance. Consultation meetings were also used to share ideas about promoting a child's social growth, and these meetings sometimes resulted in a classroom- or home-based intervention plan. These plans commonly included a contract or agreement between the child and his parent and/or teacher. Figure 10 shows a sample reward contract from the Wisconsin Early Intervention Program.

During the project period, consultation was provided to teachers of

REWARD CONTRACT

Parent/Teacher _____ Date _____

Child _____

Each time _____

Good Behavior _____

_____

_____ will get a check in a
circle at the right. When there are _____ checks,
_____ will get this Reward:

Reward: _____

When?: _____

With Whom?: _____

Where?: _____

What?: _____

The Reward for Good Behavior will be given only
after the number of checks stated above are at the
right.

Signed: Parent/Teacher _____

Child _____

Figure 10

101 participating children. The average number of teacher consultation
contacts per participating child was 3.3. Consultation was also provided to
parents of 37 of these children. When parent consultation did take place,
the average number of contacts per child was 1.4.

The Wisconsin Early Intervention social skills group modules were
the basis of—and, with few exceptions, equivalent to—the Social Growth
Program modules. These modules outlined short-term educational in-

terventions to be implemented with small groups of children. The skill-building modules were adapted from those designed by Michelson et al. (1983) for a somewhat older group of children and from those used in the Cincinnati Social Skills Development Program (Kirschenbaum et al., 1983). Each group was composed of four to five children and met on a weekly basis for 45 to 50 minutes. Participating children were offered 24 social skills group sessions, although some children met their goals and rotated out of the groups.

Our ability to teach large numbers of children social skills was possible given our use of trained and supervised paraprofessionals. These paraprofessionals were recruited from the school community and completed approximately 45 hours of training on child development, child relationship building, child management, child abuse/neglect, cultural/sexual stereotypes, and confidentiality. Information on the recruitment, training, and supervision of paraprofessionals is included in Chapter 7.

Pre- and Postevaluation

A number of assessment instruments were used to assess the effectiveness of the Wisconsin Early Intervention Program. Our overriding aim was to assess the perceptions of multiple informants before and after the program was implemented. The *Teacher-Child Rating Scale* (T-CRS), described earlier in this chapter, was used to assess teacher perceptions of children's behavior problems and competencies (Hightower et al., 1986). Parent perceptions of the children's problems and competencies were assessed with the *Child Behavior Checklist* (CBC; Achenbach & Edelbrock, 1983). This checklist includes 118 behavior problem items that are scored on a three-point scale. Complete pre- and postintervention ratings were completed by parents of 50 percent of participating children.

Although the paraprofessional social skill group leaders were obviously not "blind" to children's experimental condition, we also assessed their perceptions of the social behaviors of children in the "Full Service" condition. These group leaders completed the *Aide-Child Rating Scale* (A-CRS) (Hightower & Cowen, 1984) after two weeks of the social skills groups and consultation services. This two-week period gave them an opportunity to get to know the children well enough to complete ratings. They completed ratings again at the close of the program. The A-CRS was scored in keeping with four factors: Shy-Anxious, Initiative/Participation, Behavioral Limits, and Self-Confidence.

Wisconsin Early Intervention Program staff also participated in the pre- and postevaluation of children who obtained "Full Services" or "Partial Services" in one school. The *Children's Depression Rating Scale–Revised* (CDRS–R), a semistructured interview scale consisting of 17 items that are scored from 1 to 5 or 1 to 7, was used to assess children's feelings, thoughts, and behaviors related to depression (Poznanski et al., 1984). As reported in

King and Kirschenbaum (1990), a reliability assessment was conducted for three of the four factors and interrater agreement was adequate for two of these factors, Mood and Somatic.

Findings

Did people's perceptions of children's social behaviors change, in a positive direction, as a result of children's participation in the Wisconsin Early Intervention Program? Our findings were mixed but certainly encouraging. When significant changes in perceptions occurred, these changes were in a positive direction. Our primary findings will be presented here, and the reader is referred to King and Kirschenbaum (1990) for details concerning statistical analyses.

The *Children's Depression Rating Scale–Revised* (CDRS–R) was reliably administered to children in the "Full Services" and "Partial Services" conditions both pre- and postintervention. The interviewer was not involved in the provision of Wisconsin Early Intervention Program services and was kept blind to children's experimental condition. We found that children who participated in social skills groups in addition to consultation services made significantly greater gains than did children who obtained consultation services alone. The CDRS–R is comprehensive in its coverage of behaviors, thoughts, and feelings related to depression (e.g., school performance, social isolation, depressed mood, self-worth), and the gains made by children in the "Full Services" condition were particularly evident on the Depressed Mood factor of the CDRS–R (see Table 2 for a presentation of mean CDRS–R factor scores for the "Full Service" and "Partial Service" participants pre- and postintervention).

The social skills group leader ratings of "Full Service" children's behaviors within social skills groups also revealed significant improvements

Table 2   Children's Depression Rating Scale–Revised (CDRS–R): Means (and Standard Deviations) on Factor Scores Pre- and Postintervention

CDRS–R Factor		Full service (n = 21)	Partial service (n = 25)
Behavioral			
	Pre	4.1 (1.4)	3.5 (0.8)
	Post	3.1 (0.7)	3.1 (0.3)
Somatic			
	Pre	8.4 (2.7)	7.8 (1.9)
	Post	6.7 (1.4)	6.6 (1.7)
Mood			
	Pre	6.4 (2.3)	5.4 (1.6)
	Post	4.2 (0.6)	5.0 (2.3)

Note: High scores are associated with higher levels of depressive symptoms on each of the factors. Reprinted with permission from *Journal of Community Psychology*, Vol. 18, April 1990, p. 171.

across the intervention period. This improvement was evident on the two nonbehavioral factors of the *Aide-Child Rating Scale* (A-CRS) with adequate interrater reliability, initiative/participation, and self-confidence. Although it seems to suggest positive changes associated with participation in the social skills groups, this finding is difficult to interpret because the social skills group leaders were not "blind" observers; they were actively involved in the delivery of Wisconsin Early Intervention services. Also, because these ratings were based on observed behaviors within social skills groups, a comparison group is not available for these data.

Teacher and parent perceptions of children's behaviors pre- and postintervention, as measured by the *Teacher-Child Rating Scale* and the *Child Behavior Checklist* (CBC), did not vary as a function of experimental condition. Rather, significant improvements were found across the program period for all groups. T-CRS ratings revealed improvements across groups on four factors: Shy/Anxious, Learning Skills, Assertive Social Skills, and Task Orientation. Greater improvements were found for older participants (third-fourth grade versus first-second grade) on one factor, Frustration Tolerance. According to parent reports on the CBC, program participants showed decreases in numbers of behavior problems across the program period regardless of experimental group.

Conclusions

The evaluation of the Wisconsin Early Intervention Program offered some evidence to support the efficacy of the "Full Service" condition involving social skills groups and parent/teacher consultation services. Children obtaining these services showed evidence of less depressive symptomatology postintervention, according to CDRS–R interview data. Social skills group leaders also rated these children as showing improvements in levels of social initiative and participation as well as in observed self-confidence. The evaluation also indicates, however, that regardless of level of services obtained, children consistently improved their competencies and decreased their problem behaviors across the program period. This finding was consistent across teacher, parent, and project staff informants.

These findings both highlight the importance of empirical evaluations of intervention programs and the difficulty of conducting a true experiment within a community setting. There are several possible explanations for the improvements that participants, regardless of group assignment, actually made. One possible explanation is that the project had a generally positive effect that extended beyond the assignment of children to "experimental" conditions. The paraprofessional group leaders were respected members of the community who were in the school daily. These people talked about the program and its goals with teachers in the lunchroom and worked hard to promote a consideration of young children's social as well as academic development. Wisconsin Early Intervention Program staff also reported on the program and its goals and offered ideas for promoting children's social growth in the local community newspaper. As a further effort at extending gains beyond the confines of social skills group sessions, teachers were given weekly updates on social skills group sessions. These updates included parallel suggestions on how the concepts and skills introduced in the social skills groups could be promoted with all children in the classroom.

There are other possible explanations for the generally positive effects across time, and, most likely, a combination of factors came into play. Certain developmental changes in cognitive abilities and social behaviors would be expected across any program period with young elementary school children. Behaviors such as learning to play cooperatively and cope with frustration improve as children make a transition to less egocentric thinking and learn more adaptive social behaviors. Some of the social adjustment problems reflected slight developmental lags rather than qualitative differences in children's behaviors. These children would be expected to "catch up" or at least show gains as they developed new cognitive abilities and obtained more school socialization experiences.

Unfortunately, the funding cycle for the Wisconsin Early Intervention Program was not well timed with the academic school year. Because we chose to conduct an intensive, four-month intervention program, we were severely limited in the time available for preintervention assessments and were not able to complete behavioral observations of participants. Some evidence suggests that ratings may be insensitive to change over short time periods, as they tend to be highly influenced by reputation factors (e.g., Nelson & Carson, 1988). Consequently, we recommend that program evaluations, whenever possible, include a combination of rating scale, interview, and observational data.

SUMMARY

Proactive, schoolwide screening or more informal and individualized referral methods work effectively in identifying children for Social Growth Program services. Depending on time and personnel resources, we have found that it's helpful to include interview, questionnaire, and observations in the assessment of referred children. This three-part package enables program coordinators, therapists, and group leaders to carefully consider the perceptions of key informants (parents, teachers), the child's own report, and their own observations of what actually occurs within an environmental context. With this information, individualized and developmentally appropriate social growth goals can be comfortably established.

Assessment is one key to implementing an effective, individualized intervention. It is also critical to conducting a meaningful program evaluation. The Wisconsin Early Intervention Program evaluation described in this chapter provided encouraging evidence for the effectiveness of social skills groups. It also highlighted some of the strengths and weaknesses of particular assessment tools as well as the difficulties of carrying out "true" experiments within a community; namely, total experimental control over children's lives during an intervention program is neither possible nor desirable. Children are rapidly developing new skills and ways of thinking and they encounter a multitude of individuals and new experiences during a program period.

6

SOCIAL GROWTH
PROGRAM MODULES

The Social Growth Program consists of nine modules that can be integrated into an intervention program for individual children or small groups of children. Each module includes specific ideas for structured interventions that teach children social skill concepts, provide opportunities for practice, emphasize positive feedback, and encourage the generalization of new social skills (or levels of comfort in social situations) to other settings. Because we strongly believe that these interventions are most effective when implemented within the context of a warm and supportive relationship, many ideas are also included on building and maintaining good working relationships with children. We hope that you are able to share our optimism about young children's capacities for social and emotional growth. These Social Growth Program modules were designed to assist you in your efforts to empower children and help them learn what they can so to improve their relationships with others. Good luck!

MODULE ONE:

Who Am I?

GOALS

- ❏ Communicate purpose and structure of sessions
- ❏ Build a comfortable, nonthreatening group or individual intervention setting
- ❏ Support each child as a unique, growing person with strengths on which to build

---

RATIONALE

This module was designed to help children feel comfortable in a new setting, the one in which Social Growth Program services will be provided. Most children recommended for Social Growth Program services probably have little or no previous experience with these types of services. The unfamiliar setting may create anxiety because they do not possess the cognitive schema or set to orient them to it. The group leader or therapist's provision of *structure* and *support* can be beneficial in creating a nonthreatening atmosphere. These two kinds of reassurance will offer children the security to share concerns and try out new ways of relating to others.

The right amount of structure can diminish children's anxieties and concerns about what's going to happen. Will they be confronted or threatened? Will the group be safe? Will they know when the session is coming to a close? Will they know the other children in the group? Some of the keys to the provision of structure and a good start are: (1) clear communication about the purpose of sessions; (2) clear communication about the length and frequency of sessions; and (3) a clear, *brief* description of rules and expectancies.

Support is offered by: (1) the acceptance of a child's thoughts and feelings, (2) use of a nonthreatening, friendly tone, and (3) even pacing. Keep in mind that *how* material is presented is probably more important than *what* material is presented during initial group meetings. You may want to refer back to Chapter 4 for more information on building and maintaining positive relationships with children.

With these introductory comments aside, we need not totally ignore the content of the first session. As our goal is to support and respect each child as a unique individual, these sessions are ideally suited to talking about the topic Who Am I? Although there are many similarities among children of a given age, there are also many differences. Children can consider how they are similar and how they are different or special. What is their physical appearance and preferred style of dress? What are their favorite games and TV shows? What are their talents? Who are the special people in their lives?

Besides offering a way for group leaders and children or therapist and child to get to know each other, this module will also offer children the chance to learn via modeling. Group leaders can model their support for individual differences and encourage children to do the same. This is a good start toward helping children feel good about themselves and the group. Who Am I? also serves as an introduction to the next module, Who Are We? and how do we fit together in this world?; that is, it provides for a natural transition into a discussion of social skills. How do so many unique people learn to live together in one group, classroom, neighborhood, or world?

GROUP SESSION

Preparation Ideas for the Group Session

Identifying Participants

Kindergarten–Second Grade. Name tags help children (and group leaders) feel like they belong in the group. Although introductions are usually made in any new social encounter, it's amazing how often the excitement of the moment interferes with remembering names. The name tags will assist with the memory problem and prevent the "no one is talking to anyone in particular" problem. Construction paper cut out in the shape of favorite animals (e.g., dinosaurs) or characters (e.g., Teenage Mutant Ninja Turtles) are favorites with these younger children.

Second–Fourth Grade.   As with younger children, name tags are helpful but can be relatively straightforward for this age group. You can also take advantage of the reading skills of this age group and provide a poster with names of the group leaders and children. This poster might even be designed with enough extra space to allow for the addition of "action snapshots" of each child at some later date.

Communicating Rules and Expectancies

Kindergarten–Second Grade.   Posters can help orient children to the structure of Social Growth Program group sessions. They can help in communicating the idea of confidentiality. That is, although young children are certainly not bound by confidentiality, the idea is planted that the group is a special, safe setting with its own set of norms. Posters can also help communicate information about session times and group rules.

1. Confidentiality
   REMEMBER
   WHAT WE SAY HERE
   WHAT WE SEE HERE
   WHAT WE HEAR HERE
   LET IT STAY HERE

2. Group Rules

DO	*DO NOT*
SMILE	RUN
LISTEN	KICK
SHARE	THROW THINGS

3. Meeting Times
   Clocks can be made depicting the times group sessions begin and end. These can be drawn on a poster or made from paper plates with fasteners.

Second–Fourth Grade.   Posters, blackboard lists, or written handouts can be helpful when communicating group rules. Topics could include confidentiality (rhyme listed under preparation ideas for younger children); group rules; and meeting start, clean-up, and end times.

"How We're Alike" Activities

Kindergarten–Second Grade.   A poster that depicts similarities among children in the group can serve as an icebreaker, particularly for more reticent or anxious children. There are many possibilities here. Consider a photo of the school or community, magazine pictures of ice cream, candy, toys, a "First Grade" sign, or pictures of children doing schoolwork. It helps to remember that feeling "different" can be very threatening to all of us, but particularly to young children in new group settings. Thus, understanding commonalities is a nice way to start.

Second–Fourth Grade.   Brainstorming works well with children in this age group. It involves accepting (not evaluating) all thoughts or ideas about a topic. Using a large tablet or blackboard, group leaders can challenge the children to create a long list. If children are unfamiliar with brainstorming or have trouble generating ideas, group leaders can model the activity. Commonalities to keep in mind include membership in a school community, similar school tasks or assignments, some overwhelmingly favorite movies or TV shows, and general characteristics of human beings.

"How I'm Unique" Activities

Kindergarten–Second Grade. Kindergarten through second-grade children are, as a group, more comfortable with drawing, pasting, and cutting activities than with writing activities. Children might draw pictures or cut pictures out of magazines that fit any of the following "I Am Special" themes: *I Look Like Me, I Like to Do Lots of Things,* or *These Things Remind Me of My Home.* Cut and paste collages might be titled *My Favorite Foods* (or *Animals, Things to Do, Places*). Group leaders can encourage children to describe themselves, their likes and dislikes, and their hobbies.

Second–Fourth Grade.   There are many options with this age group. The ideas for kindergarten–second-grade children (e.g., *I Am Special* posters) are good possibilities. These older children could also make a *Words that Describe Me* collage, cutting out words from magazines. They could

make a *My Favorite* _____ collage that combined pictures and words. Another possibility is the use of ditto worksheets titled *All About Me, My Favorites, I Can,* and so on that ask children to tell about themselves.

Guidelines for Conducting the Group Session: Who Am I?

General Introduction

At the beginning of this first session, group leaders should try to greet children as they enter the room and welcome them into the group. After this, name tags and introductions are helpful. As group leaders begin to describe the purpose and structure of group sessions (hopefully using some of the props described in the preparation section), a friendly tone and even pacing of material helps. The group purpose, rules, and time frame are best communicated before going on to the remainder of this module. In explaining confidentiality, it is helpful to emphasize that group conversations are meant to be private. The group leaders can state that they will not repeat these private conversations to a child's parents, teachers, or friends unless they need to protect someone's safety. Group leaders instruct children to respect the privacy of other group members as well.

How We're Alike

Introduction.   This section can be introduced in more than one way, although a general guide might be as follows:

We have six people in our group, four children and two adults. We

are all alike in many ways. We are all people. We are all in _____

_____ elementary school in the city of _____

_____. We will all be meeting together twice each week. Let's think of some other ways in which we are all alike.

Modeling.   Group leaders can take turns suggesting ways in which members are alike. Acceptance and realistic praise of all ideas should be modeled for the children (see the preparation ideas for the group session earlier). After taking turns offering and accepting a few ideas, children can be encouraged to join in the activity. It would probably not be a good idea to press children to participate. Children who do participate, however, should be given positive feedback for their ideas as well as for their acceptance of others' ideas.

How I'm Unique

Introduction.   This section might be introduced as follows:

We are also different in many ways. Who Am I? Who Are You? We have a lot in common but we're not *exactly* the same. Let's see if we can get to know each other as unique, one-of-a-kind people. We are all different and thereby special in some ways. Now, to help us learn about ourselves and each other, let's talk about some ways that we're different.

Modeling.   Group leaders can begin in a nonthreatening way by talking about differences between people who are not present in the room. Posters or magazine pictures that depict different people in different places can be used. As a second step, group leaders themselves can identify the ways they differ from each other (e.g., size, clothing, voice pitch). The third step might involve children in a discussion of the ways group leaders differ from each other. This can lead into a discussion on the ways the children differ from each other (e.g., names, eye color, size). Appropriate, nonaggressive comments are to be encouraged and supported. Positive feedback is given to all participants.

Because the group leaders and children may realistically not know each other well enough to get beyond a discussion of physical differences, some of the preparation ideas suggested earlier would be helpful here. To the extent that children offer the group (perhaps via a poster, collage, or completed ditto) information about their personal preferences, talents, and pleasures, a more meaningful discussion can occur.

Group Discussion

This is an opportunity to regroup at a discussion table and summarize the main points of the module; share children's collages, pictures, or written products; and offer positive feedback. The positive feedback can be specifically offered to children for brainstorming similarities, pointing out others' differences, describing personal differences, and listening to and accepting the comments of others. This last section of the session is also an opportunity to explain and discuss the FOR ME homework assignment as well as the FOR MY PARENTS AND TEACHERS handout.

Social Growth Program

Module One: Who Am I?
For Me

1. Bring in a snapshot of yourself next time. It could be a recent one or one from when you were a baby or a small child.

2. Find and bring in a snapshot or magazine picture of two or more people together. They could be eating, talking, sitting, playing, or working.

Social Growth Program

Module One: Who Am I?
For My Parents and Teachers

Child's Name _____

Group Leaders' Names _____

Today's Date _____

     Today's session presented the message that each of us is a unique, growing person with personal strengths on which to build. Children reviewed how they are alike and also talked about how

each of them is unique. They made _____ and shared these with other group members. These activities helped us get to know each other and become comfortable working together as a group. They also served as a basis to our upcoming Who Are We? group session; that is, given our individual differences, how do we learn to get along in this world? This will start us on our way toward improving our social skills.

Additional Comments:

INDIVIDUAL SESSION

Preparation Ideas for the Individual Session

Identifying Participants

Name tags are usually unnecessary in the more personalized individual session. Younger children who are just learning to read (and *can easily* read their own name), however, might enjoy a nametag for themselves and for the therapist, too.

Communicating Rules and Expectancies

Expectancies can usually be verbalized clearly during individual sessions in such a way that the preparation of additional material is unnecessary. It's possible for the therapist to "tune in" with one child and evaluate the extent to which the child really hears and understands expectancies. Because rules are probably best deemphasized in individual sessions, these expectancies are probably minimal (e.g., "Be in office with me for 50 minutes"). With these younger children, it might be helpful to depict meeting times (session start and end times) visually. This could be done on a small poster or on a clock made from paper plates with fasteners.

Rules are even more deemphasized in individual sessions, where group behavior management is not an issue. Basic information on confidentiality can be provided verbally. Because many or most children referred for Social Growth Program services will not have previous experience in a mental health setting, they are unaware of the meaning of confidentiality. The therapist can be fairly straightforward in telling them:

> The things that you say during our time together will not be told to others. They will not be told to your parents, teachers, brother, or anyone else. But there is one exception to this general rule. I cannot keep your words private if I have reason to believe that you or someone else might be physically hurt. Then I will need to get some help.

"How We're Alike" Activities

The absence of other children in the office offers a challenge to the therapist or mental health professional. The task becomes one of defining "How are most kids alike?" and imagery may be helpful, something like, for example, "Consider some of your friends at school. Let's see if we can describe some things about them. . . ." Children can be helped to brainstorm ideas about how they are similar to other children (membership in school community, shared homework assignments, favorite after-school activities, size, etc.).

The individual therapist or mental health professional does not work in a setting that directly confronts children with how they are "different" from other children. Nevertheless, fears of "being different" are sometimes lurking, and it helps to deal with them before moving on to the How I'm Unique section. This can be done by acknowledging a child's similarities with other children as well as the ways in which he or she belongs to a world of young children. Certain props used in the group sessions might also be helpful here.

"How I'm Unique" Activities

The "How I'm Unique" preparation ideas for group sessions are also useful for individual sessions. Although these structured activities may be unnecessary, especially with highly verbal children, many children are action-oriented. These children may speak more freely if they are engaged at the same time in a related task.

Guidelines for Conducting the Individual Session

A few comments are in order about the format of individual sessions. Although the module topic (e.g., Who Am I?), and its rationale are similar, the format of these sessions differs from that of group sessions. The major reason for this is, quite simply, the absence of other children. The fact that the focus of the Social Growth Program is on interpersonal behavior presents a creative challenge to the individual therapist. This therapist will sometimes role-play (or, act the part of) a child, use imagery, and use other props to "bring to interpersonal life" the activities within the sessions. Although the provision of structure and support are still important in building a therapeutic relationship with the child, less structure is needed in individual sessions. The room is often smaller, group behavior management concerns are absent, and the therapist can pay careful attention to the responses of the individual child.

General Introduction

After welcoming the child in a friendly tone, the therapist can describe the purpose and nature of the sessions. The therapist might describe their length, the approximate number that he or she expects to take place, and their general format. It's also a good idea to explain carefully what is meant by confidentiality. One way to present this concept is described under Preparation Ideas for the group session.

How We're (Most Kids) Alike

There are several ways for the therapist to communicate the message that he or she accepts the child as someone who belongs to the universe of children. Here the notion of belonging is really the guiding concept. Photos, drawing, and magazine pictures work well, as do imagery and brainstorming with older children. Wandering through pictures and drawings with a child, the therapist can make a game out of finding similarities among children (and sometimes among all people, including the therapist!).

How I'm Unique.   This section can begin with an easy transition from focusing on similarities among people to focusing on their differences. The emphasis is on the positive, special aspects of each person. The child can describe himself by making and telling about an "I Am Special" poster, "Words that Describe Me" collage, or any of a number of possible cut-and-paste collages.

Discussion.   The therapist should summarize, with the child's help, the main points of the module and offer positive feedback to the child for sharing himself and working with the therapist. Some time should be saved to discuss the FOR ME homework assignment and FOR MY PARENTS handout (This can be modified to a FOR MY PARENTS AND TEACHERS handout if the therapist is working within a school setting or has the parents' permission to share information with the child's teachers.) The FOR ME homework assignment is given in the group sessions section.

Social Growth Program

Module One: Who Am I?
For My Parents

Child's Name _____

Leader's Name _____

Today's Date _____

    Today's session presented the message that each of us is a unique, growing person with personal strengths on which to build. We

discussed what _____ has in common with other

children as well as ways in which _____ differs

from other children. We also worked on an activity (_____

_____), which helped us get to know each other and become comfortable working together. This also served as a basis to our upcoming Who Are We? session; that is, given our individual differences, how do we learn to get along in this world? This will start us on our way toward improving our social skills.

Additional Comments:

MODULE TWO:

Who Are We?
What Are Social Skills?

GOALS

- ❑ Introduce the meaning and importance of social skills
- ❑ Identify and praise each child's present social skills

RATIONALE

Module Two introduces children to the concept of social skills and helps each child identify his or her existing social skills. Some children will also be able to take a part in setting their own social skill goals.

Social implies interpersonal, involving interactions with one other or many other persons. When we consider the daily lives of children, it is clear that much of what they do or achieve occurs within a social context or setting (e.g., bus ride, reading group, lunch line, classroom instruction, meal time, grocery shopping). Children, like adults, are social beings who do not exist in a vacuum. Children's responses in these settings often affect others' behaviors toward them, which in turn affect their own feelings and behaviors.

Social skills are social, interpersonal behaviors that tend to evoke positive outcomes. *Skills* implies that these social behaviors can and should be taught in a systematic, goal-directed manner. Thus, there is no need to rely on random, chance forces to promote positive, adaptive social behaviors. Children are not born with social skills and they do not necessarily acquire them on their own. Nevertheless, the socially skilled child is better prepared to develop and thrive in our complex social world.

GROUP SESSION

Preparation Ideas for the Group Session

Introducing Social Skills

Kindergarten–Second Grade.   Magazine pictures can be used to make social skill poster boards. These poster boards might depict skills such as *listening, cooperating,* and *sharing.* The poster boards facilitate children's understanding and identification of social skills during the session. It is sometimes easier for children to realize what skills they already have if you show them the opposite. During the introduction phase of the module, group leaders might pantomime or role-play poor social skills (refusal to share, poor listening, or playing a mouse who doesn't stand up for his rights). This could be done in an exaggerated, comical manner. Puppets might also be used to model social skills or a lack of social skills.

Second–Fourth Grade.   Social skills poster boards made from magazine pictures might also be used with these older children. Group leaders might also plan to do some pantomimes or role-plays of good and poor social skills during the introduction section of the module. Group leaders should consider ahead of time some situations that might be particularly relevant for the age group with whom they are working. Taking turns in a board game with stated rules, for example, is important for most second-through fourth-grade children. Puppets might also be used to present material in a varied, light-hearted way.

Modeling Social Skills

Kindergarten–Second Grade.   Group leaders should plan to have a large tablet ready to record social skills that group leaders and children display during the introduction. After the children have been introduced to the concept of social skills and the importance of social skills, group leaders can help them to identify and list their own social skills. Some of the children will not be able to read so it is important to make clear verbal statements when adding items to the list. In preparation for the modeling phase of the group session, they should also try to bring in a game that the children can play together during the session. Games should be easy for the age group and capable of being finished within a short period of time (e.g., a simple card game).

Second–Fourth Grade.   The materials required for the modeling phase of group sessions are a large tablet for a brainstorming activity and some age-appropriate games. For this age group, possibilities include simple board games that involve overcoming obstacles as children race to move playing pieces from start to finish or simple card games (e.g., rummy). If group leaders are able to bring in these materials, additional preparation is not needed for this session.

Guidelines for Conducting the Group Session

Introducing Social Skills

The module might be introduced in this way:

We are all unique and special in some ways. As we discussed in our last session (Who Am I?), we have differing looks, homes, favorite games, and talents. Let's look at some of the pictures that you brought in. [*Note the pictures the children brought in as their homework assignment for Module One.*] What activities are depicted in the pictures of different children? How do the pictures suggest that each child is special or unique in some way? [*Work with the children to identify the differences between them as a review of Module One.*]

Given these many differences, how do we all manage to live together in one world? We see other people when we get up in the morning, when we ride to school, when we sit in class, when we eat lunch, and when we go places like stores, playgrounds and movies. How do we manage to get what we want, do what we want, and feel comfortable with all these other people around? This brings us to *social skills*. [*It might be helpful to write these words on the chalk board or a large tablet.*] *Social* means with one or more other people. We are social when we are talking, working, or playing with other people. We are not being social when we are sleeping, taking a shower, or reading a book alone in our rooms. A *skill* is something that we've learned to do well. We all have many skills. These might be reading, riding a bike, eating with silverware or washing our own clothes. We did not know how to do these things when we were born. These are skills that we have learned since we were born.

So what are social skills? They are skilled, learned ways of behaving with and responding to other people. Let's consider an example. [*Present a poster board depicting a particular skill, such as listening or cooperating.*] What social skill do you see in this picture? [*Repeat with another poster board.*] If you would like to use puppet portrayals of social skills, that would fit in well here. This might be particularly helpful with younger age groups. [*If children were given the Module One FOR ME assignment to bring in a picture of two or more people together, these pictures are used in this discussion.*]

Finally, why are social skills important? They help us get along with others, make friends more easily, join in on fun games, ask questions when we are confused, and stay out of trouble. When we are happier and better able to communicate, it is easier to do our schoolwork, too.

Modeling Social Skills

1. Modeling Between Group Leaders.   Group leaders have been showing or modeling a number of social skills during the introduction phase of the module. At this time, group leaders need to identify, describe, and praise each other's social skills. These could be listed on a large tablet. Examples of skills that were probably modeled during the introduction and discussion include active listening, asking questions, taking turns, and positive messages.

2. Modeling Between Group Leader and Children.   Group leaders describe and praise children's social skills as well. These might also be listed. Children have probably been listening carefully, sitting cooperatively, and not interrupting each other. Some positive social skill should be noted and praised for *each* child.

3. Modeling Among Children.   A fun way for children to see and be praised for existing social skills is to have them play a simple card game or short board game together. Allow approximately 5 to 15 minutes for the game and describe and praise observed social skills. Facilitate a discussion during which children can identify and acknowledge each other's social skills.

Group Discussion

The discussion can be used to sum up the meaning of social skills and review the skills that were observed during the session. Group leaders should praise generously, then introduce the idea that we all have more to learn and that we need practice with different kinds of social skills: some of us may need more practice with skills such as active listening, whereas others may need more practice with taking turns or sharing. Group leaders should be sure to leave time to discuss the FOR ME homework assignment and distribute the FOR MY PARENTS AND TEACHERS handout.

Social Growth Program

Module Two: Who Are We? What Are Social Skills?
For Me

1. Choose a time when you are doing something with other people. It might be eating dinner, watching TV, or riding a bus. Make a list of people's social skills during this time.

2. Think about your own social skills. Write down two or three skills you would like to improve on.

3. Play a game with someone in your family, neighborhood, or classroom. It could be a card game, a board game, a computer game, or even a basketball game. Make a list of the social skills you observe during the game. Which of these skills were necessary to play the game together?

Social Growth Program

Module Two: Who Are We?
What Are Social Skills?
For My Parents and Teachers

Child's Name _____

Group Leaders' Names _____

Today's Date _____

     Today's session presented the message that we can learn skills that will help us to get along with other people and be more comfortable with other people. We call them *social skills*. We are all unique and special or different in some ways, yet we must learn to live with others. Social skills help us to get along with others. We are not born with these skills, but we can learn them.

     During our session, children took note of and were praised for the many social skills they already have. Children described and showed these many different skills during a game that required active listening, asking questions, and taking turns. We also talked about skills that we could improve upon. After identifying our own social

skill goals, we will begin practicing one specific skill, _____

_____, during our next session.

Additional Comments:

INDIVIDUAL SESSION

Preparation Ideas for the Individual Session

Introducing Social Skills

Kindergarten–Second Grade.   Individual sessions do not require the same degree of preparation as group sessions. Preparation might consist of finding and bringing in magazines and poster board materials. Then the therapist might create social skills poster boards with the child during the session. Another preparation idea for individual sessions is as simple as bringing in one or two puppets. These puppets could then be used during the session to introduce the concept of social skills. The puppets could be used to model either positive social skills such as sharing or listening or an absence of social skills. Sometimes it is fun to do this in an exaggerated, comical manner. This is also helpful in building rapport during early sessions.

Second–Fourth Grade.   Individual sessions with second- through fourth-grade children are similar to those with younger children in rarely requiring the same amount of preparation as group sessions. Once again, it would be helpful for the therapist to bring magazines or posters into the session to work with the child in identifying pictures of people listening, cooperating with each other, or talking with each other. Puppets can also be used effectively in individual sessions.

Modeling Social Skills

Very little preparation is needed for the modeling section of this module. The therapist may choose to bring in a simple game that she can play with the child and have some paper available for making a list of observed social skills.

Guidelines for Conducting the Individual Session

Introducing Social Skills

You may recall from Module One that the format of individual sessions differs from that of group sessions in usually requiring less structure for individual sessions. It also differs in allowing the therapist to pay careful attention to the special needs and unique responses of the individual child. It would be helpful to begin Module Two with some acknowledgement and discussion of the Module One homework assignment. If the child brings a snapshot of himself or a magazine picture of people together, the therapist might begin with a conversation about these. The continuing effort to build a warm, trusting relationship with the child will require even pacing, active listening, and a sensitivity to the child. While looking at the snapshot with the child, the therapist might comment on the ways in which the child is similar to others his or her age, as well as the unique and positive things that are the child's own special characteristics. If the child has brought in a snapshot of two or more people together, the child could work with the therapist to identify ways in which the people in the snapshot are different and ways in which they are similar. This could lead into a discussion of how different people learn to get along with each other.

The therapist can then introduce the concept of *social skills*. This could be introduced in the same way that it is introduced in group sessions; that is, the therapist can explain that *social* means with one or more other people and give examples of when we are being social and when we are not being social. The therapist can explain that a skill is something that we have learned to do well. The child can probably identify one or more of his or her own skills, and the therapist can point out that the child probably did not know how to do these things when he or she was born; skills are usually things we have learned since we were born. Examples might include tying shoes, memorizing a poem, reading a story, or riding a bike. Then, to tie together the concepts of *social* and *skills*, the therapist can explain that social skills are skilled ways of behaving with or responding to other people. At this point, the therapist might want to use the materials that he brought to the session and prepare a poster board or a collage with the child that illustrates a particular social skill. The therapist might also want to use puppet portrayals of social skills.

Identifying Child's Social Skills

The therapist can begin by identifying the child's social skills during the session. These might be listed on a piece of paper and discussed. Examples of skills that many of the children will have displayed include active listening, asking questions, and cooperating; each and every child has some positive social skill that can be identified and praised. The therapist might then play a simple card game or board game with the child. This creates a good opportunity to identify and praise the social skills that the child shows during the game. Toward the end of an individual session, there's an opportunity for a general discussion about the child's own situation. This might involve a discussion of the child's difficulty with peers, siblings, parents, or teachers. It might be possible for the therapist to begin to work with the child to identify the child's strengths and difficulties alike in the area of social skills.

Social Growth Program

Module Two: Who Are We? What Are Social Skills?
For My Parents

Child's Name _____

Group Leader's Names _____

Today's Date _____

During our session today, we talked about *Social Skills*. These are skills that will help us get along with other people and be more comfortable with other people. Although we are all unique or different in some ways, we must learn to live with others. Social skills help us to get along with others. We are not born with these skills, but we can learn them.

We identified some social skills that _____

already has learned to do well. These included _____

_____

_____ showed these skills during our activ-

ity today, which was _____ . We also talked about

skills that _____ could improve upon. We will

begin practicing one specific skill, _____ , during
our next session.

Additional Comments:

MODULE THREE:

Active Listening

GOALS

❏ Introduce children to the importance of listening carefully to others' messages
❏ Practice and improve active listening skills such as eye contact and concentration

RATIONALE

Active listening requires that we work carefully to understand the spoken messages of others. It demands that we tune in and concentrate on those messages.

Active listening is one of the most important social skills that children will learn. It helps them to (1) minimize confusion about assignments, tasks, game rules; (2) have better two-way conversations; (3) understand other children's concerns and feelings; and (4) show an interest in other children. Because active listening is such an essential part of good communication, it is closely related to acceptance among peers.

GROUP SESSION

Preparation Ideas for the Group Session

Introducing Active Listening Skills

Kindergarten–Second Grade. As a way of introducing the *importance of active listening*, the group leaders might prepare pantomimes that demonstrate what happens in a variety of situations when children do not listen.

Another option would be to use puppets to demonstrate these same situations. Possible situations are:

- Three children are going to play a game such as Chutes and Ladders. One child knows the game and offers to teach the others, but one of the other children looks around the room and does not listen. Show what happens when the game starts.

- Some children are having a conversation about their favorite TV shows. One child doesn't listen and asks things that don't fit into the conversation. This disrupts the conversation. The other children might be less likely to include the nonlistening child the next time.

- One child is crying on the playground and tells another child, "I was running. I fell down and twisted my foot. It hurts." The other child says, "Don't be a crybaby," and runs off.

Some additional materials would be helpful in presenting the skills involved in Active Listening. Group leaders might bring magazine pictures of people talking and listening to each other. These can be displayed one at a time while children comment on how they can tell whether or not one person is listening to another person. If the group leaders also bring a large tablet or have the use of a chalkboard, they can make a list of the Active Listening skills, which will be a useful reference during the modeling sections of the session:

> ### STOP OTHER ACTIVITIES
> ### LOOK AT PERSON
> ### CONCENTRATE, TRY TO UNDERSTAND

Second–Fourth Grade.   Group leaders might begin by having children offer their ideas of why it is important to listen carefully. The children's ideas might be listed on a large tablet. It is important to be nonjudgmental and list all of their comments. As a second step, puppets or pantomimes could be used to illustrate the importance of active listening. The possible situations that were listed under the preparation ideas for younger children could be used with slight modifications; an age-appropriate game, for example, might be Bingo rather than Chutes and Ladders. One additional active listening skill is presented to this older group of children. Because this skill requires some explanation, it would be helpful to prepare and begin with a list of the four active listening skills:

> ### STOP OTHER ACTIVITIES
> ### LOOK AT PERSON
> ### CONCENTRATE, TRY TO UNDERSTAND
> ### MAKE A RELATED COMMENT

Magazine pictures of people talking and listening to each other might also be used. Children could observe and describe the listed skills as they are displayed in the pictures.

Modeling Active Listening Skills

Kindergarten–Fourth Grade.   A number of fun activities can enable children to observe active listening skills in themselves and in others. One idea is to use a game. A good game for young children is "I'm going to grandmother's house and I am taking with me a _____ ." The first player names one object, the second player names the same object plus a new one. This recital continues with each player repeating all objects in order and then adding a new one.

A second possible activity is a short, time-limited conversation about a chosen topic (e.g., favorite sport). This activity offers a good chance to give children feedback concerning their listening skills. Finally, the group leaders might choose a fun game or craft that they could teach children to do with just a few simple instructions, such as braiding a friendship bracelet.

Guidelines for Conducting the Group Session

Introducing Active Listening Skills

The module might be introduced in this way:

> Listening is one of the most important social skills we will practice. It is important because we must listen carefully before we can understand assignments, understand stories, have good conversations, ask good questions, and understand what others are feeling. Let's look at what can happen when we *do not* listen carefully. [*See the preparation ideas earlier.*]
> Listening is like hearing, but it is harder than hearing. Listening means hearing plus concentrating on what we are hearing. It means trying hard to understand what someone else is saying.

Kindergarten–Second Grade.   Group leaders could say:

Let's look at some pictures of people talking with each other [*See the preparation ideas earlier.*] What do we see? [*Offer hints that help children to identify the three skills: Stop Other Activities, Look at Person, and Concentrate.*]

Second–Fourth Grade.   Although the first three active listening skills are self-explanatory, the final skill, Make a Related Comment, requires more explanation. By making a related comment, the listener communicates that she is interested and concerned. The comment also shows that the listener is trying to understand what is being said and wants to make sure that she does understand. Of the various ways to make these related comments, we will describe two possibilities. One is to reflect back what was said—for example, "I hear you saying. . . ." Another is to repeat the speaker's statement in the form of a question—for example, one child says, "I don't like spinach," and the listener replies, "Spinach isn't your favorite vegetable?" You may want to practice just one of these ways with the children by reviewing many different examples.

Modeling Active Listening Skills

Between Group Leaders.   Group leaders can begin by modeling the listening skills that they have listed in bold letters. They might do this with a brief, friendly conversation about some of their school activities. Another possibility would be for one group leader to teach the other group leader a new skill, such as how to play a simple card game or how to use flour and salt to make play-dough. Again, it is important that only a few steps are required and that the conversation can be brief. After each situation group leaders should review and discuss, with the children's help, how they stopped other activities, looked at each other, concentrated, and made a related comment.

Between Group Leaders and Children.   Similar situations can be used between group leaders and children to demonstrate listening skills. Group leaders can take turns having a short conversation with each of the children in the group. These conversations should be structured in such a way that each group leader–child pair is given a situation or activity to discuss. This might be a favorite sport, a favorite TV show, or even a homework assignment. Group leaders could also teach the children how to make something such as a paper plane, paper hat, or braided friendship bracelet while stressing the importance of listening and concentrating.

Each child's present listening skills are praised. Group leaders should make an effort to be noncritical, for some children will need lots of practice with this module.

Between Children.   Group leaders can set up short conversations between pairs of children. Depending on group composition, they may want to provide topics, provide a number of choices, or encourage children to choose their own topics. It may be two, three, or even four sessions before children are ready for this modeling phase. Group leaders should make an effort to give positive feedback about each child's listening skills.

Group Discussion.   A group discussion is included at the end of each Active Listening session. If four sessions are spent on this module, there will be four group discussions. Each discussion will offer an opportunity to explore and reach some closure on what took place and what was learned during that session. Children can also be encouraged to ask questions and make comments about the session.

Following the first Active Listening session, group leaders should save some of the discussion time for a review of the completed FOR ME homework assignments from Module Two (Who Are We? What Are Social Skills?). These assignments and their review will help integrate concepts and skills covered in the Social Growth Program. Their review during the group discussion will also provide some continuity from session to session.

Social Growth Program

Module Three: Active Listening
For Me

1. Find and cut out two magazine pictures of people talking with each other. Paste or tape them on paper and list the Active Listening skills next to them.

2. Ask your parent, brother, or sister to tell you how to do something. Practice listening carefully. Then tell them about one of your school activities or try to teach them how to do something and observe how they listen to you.

Social Growth Program

Module Three: Active Listening
For my Parents and Teachers

Child's Name _____

Group Leaders' Names _____

Today's Date _____

     Today's session introduced children to the importance of listening carefully when other children or adults are talking to them. We call this *active listening* because it is the active process of hearing and trying to understand what is heard.

     Active listening requires that we learn to do each of the following actions:

1. Stop other activities.
2. Look at the person talking.
3. Concentrate on what is being said.
4. Ask a question to clarify what was said or make a comment to show understanding.

     We talked about how active listening helps us to understand directions, ask good questions, have good conversations with others, and understand people's feelings. Thus, active listening is one of the most important social skills. It is related to all the other skills we will practice in these sessions.

Additional Comments:

INDIVIDUAL SESSION

Preparation Ideas for the Individual Session

Individual sessions structured in keeping with the Active Listening module require little preparation. The therapist can pay careful attention to the individual child's responses and, in addition, can aim the session toward the child's developmental level. Because of the greater opportunity to fine-tune the session to an individual child's needs, separate preparation ideas are not presented for kindergarten through second grade versus second-grade through fourth-grade children. Rather, therapists can use their own judgment to individualize sessions.

Introducing Active Listening Skills

The therapist's preparation might consist of choosing activities to illustrate the active listening skills and gathering the materials required by these activities. One possibility would be to make use of puppets to demonstrate listening skills: two puppets, for example, could be used to illustrate what happens when children try to learn to play a new game together and one child does not listen. Another activity might involve listing the active listening skills on a paper or poster board and, perhaps, finding, cutting out, and discussing magazine pictures of people talking and listening to each other.

Modeling Active Listening Skills

The modeling phase of the active listening module presents the greatest challenge to the individual therapist because of the absence of multiple group members. One possibility is to agree with the child on a topic for conversation. Then the therapist and child can engage in a short, time-limited conversation about the topic. This conversation should be short enough to enable the child and the therapist to focus on their active listening skills. Following the conversation, the therapist can give the child feedback about his or her skills. Then another topic could be chosen and another conversation could take place.

Guidelines for Conducting the Individual Session

Introducing Active Listening Skills

The therapist might begin by discussing the importance of listening to many positive outcomes. These include understanding school and home-work assignments; understanding stories; and having good conversations with friends, parents, and teachers. Most children will understand the importance of listening, although they may not have been aware of the individual listening skills. The therapist can help with this part of the presentation by listing the active listening skills and demonstrating, using puppets or other activities, both the presence and the absence of active listening skills (see the preparation ideas earlier). The use of the fourth active listening skill, Make a Related Comment, should be a decision based on the child's developmental level and the number of sessions available for this module. It sometimes requires a good deal of discussion and practice for children to master this specific skill.

Modeling Active Listening Skills

It helps to begin by giving the child a chance to observe and comment on others' listening skills. This observational phase provides a meaningful learning experience and desensitizes the child to giving and being given feedback. Because individual sessions are inherently short on role models, the therapist may make use of puppets during this phase. After getting off to a good start, the therapist and child might engage in brief games or conversations that require active listening. Discussion and feedback can follow each activity.

Social Growth Program

Module Three: Active Listening
For my Parents

Child's Name _____

Leader's Name _____

Today's Date _____

　　　　Today's session introduced _____ to the importance of listening carefully when other children or adults are talking. We called this Active Listening because it is the active process of hearing and trying to understand what we have heard. Active listening requires that we learn to do each of the following:

1. Stop other activities.
2. Look at the person talking.
3. Concentrate on what is being said.
4. Ask a question to clarify what was said or make a comment to show our understanding.

　　We talked about how active listening helps us to understand directions, ask good questions, have good conversations with others, and understand people's feelings. Thus, active listening is one of the most important social skills. It is related to all the other social skills we will practice.

Additional Comments:

MODULE FOUR:

Warm Messages

Goals

❏ Help children understand how the types of messages they give affect others

❏ Practice giving "warm" or positive messages to others

RATIONALE

This module emphasizes effective communication with others. It focuses on the process of giving and receiving messages. Learning how to give messages that vary in their impact on others is an important skill. This module helps children distinguish between "warm" messages that make people feel positive and good about themselves and "cold" messages that can have opposite effects.

Children can develop more positive relationships with their peers if they understand that we are all affected by what others say to us. For example, children might learn that when they or their friends are feeling unhappy or angry, it may be because of something someone said. When children can identify the source of their feelings, they can sometimes cope with them and resolve problems more easily. Of equal importance, learning how to give warm messages can improve children's ability to get along with other children. Warm messages can initiate or maintain a positive verbal and behavioral exchange among peers, whereas negative messages may set off a conflict or end an otherwise friendly exchange.

GROUP SESSION

Preparation Ideas for the Group Session

The introduction and modeling sections of this module require little preparation. The concept of positive versus negative messages, however, can be most easily illustrated if you use some type of tangible tokens or symbols for positive and negative messages. Regardless of the age of the children in the group, we recommend that two small bags of positive and negative tokens be prepared for each group leader and child, one containing positive tokens (pieces of soft cloth, colorful paper circle cutouts, or cotton balls) and the other negative tokens (small balls of aluminum foil, bottle caps, small pieces of sandpaper). Each person in the group will need a number of positive tokens and a number of negative tokens.

Guidelines for Conducting the Group Session

Introduction

The module might be introduced in this way:

What we say to each other makes a big difference in how we feel about ourselves. Did anyone have someone say something really nice to him or her today or yesterday? [*Group leaders might want to record the positive responses on a blackboard or tablet of paper.*] How did that make you feel? Did anyone have someone say something mean to him or her yesterday or today? [*Group leaders might also want to record these responses.*] How did that make you feel? [*Group leaders might ask other group members how they would feel in each of the volunteered situations.*]

Today we are going to learn about saying things to each other that make us feel positive or warm inside. We are also going to learn about the kinds of things we say to each other that make us feel unhappy.

Group leaders can then introduce the concepts of positive, warm messages versus negative, cold messages. It is helpful to pass out the tokens of positive and negative messages while introducing these concepts. Group leaders can give examples to illustrate the effects that different kinds of messages have on others.

Modeling

1. Modeling Between Group Leaders.   Group Leader A says something positive to Group Leader B, such as, "I really enjoy working with you." As Group Leader A makes this comment, she gives Group Leader B a positive token. Group Leader B smiles warmly and says, "Why, thank you so much,

_____ (name)." Group Leader B then gives a positive token to Group Leader A.

After modeling an exchange of positive messages (and positive tokens), the group leaders should model an exchange of negative messages, this time some remark such as, "I don't like your shirt." Or something a little more personal, such as, "You mumble too much," could be introduced. Following each exchange of messages, group leaders can tell the group how they felt when they heard the message.

2. Modeling Between Group Leaders and Children.   Group leaders begin with a group brainstorming activity to generate a list of situations where one person could give a positive message to another person, then they choose and role play one of these situations, completing a positive message exchange with each child in the group. Possible role play situations include acknowledging children's accomplishments (math assignment, soccer game, science fair, piano recital), acknowledging children's helpfulness, or expressing positive, personal feelings. Role play participants should hand out a positive message token with each positive exchange and help each child respond to the positive message in an effective way. Then they choose a second situation and role-play a positive message exchange with each child. It is not a problem if the identical role-play is conducted with each child, because the repetition sometimes lowers children's anxieties besides being a good strategy for enhancing children's memory of learned material. It is important to remember to help children *receive* as well as *give* positive messages. Receiving positive messages might involve thanking the giver, smiling, or acknowledging the receipt of the positive token.

3. Modeling Between Children.   Each child, in turn, can choose one of the situations from the list generated during the brainstorming activity. The partner for the role-play can either be assigned or perhaps be determined by drawing a name from a hat. It sometimes helps to coach each child on his or her role before beginning the exchange of positive messages and tokens. (With some groups, it may be necessary to write out the script on a blackboard or large tablet.) The group leaders' task is to provide lots of positive reinforcement and some suggestions for improving the ways in which children give and receive messages. It is important to give positive feedback to each child for trying out this game in front of the group and for doing some part of it very well (and to be specific about the positive aspects). Group leaders can also suggest how the exchange might be improved, taking care to point out how the receiver of each message appeared to feel and to inquire directly about these feelings. The group leader can also involve other group members in giving feedback. Group leaders might ask children how they would have felt had they just received the same message. They can ask the other children for ideas on how to improve these messages.

Group Discussion

Group leaders ask the children what they liked best about this game. What did they learn? Did they discover something about *giving* positive messages? Negative messages? How do they usually respond when receiving positive messages? Negative messages? Did they learn something about themselves or about others in the group? Group leaders review the FOR MY PARENTS AND TEACHERS handout and remind children to show these to their parents and teachers and to complete the FOR ME paper. (Group leaders will need to attach a positive token to each of the FOR ME papers. Good possibilities include stickers, cotton balls, or paper stars.)

Social Growth Program

Module Four: Warm Messages
For Me

1. Give out one of the attached positive tokens along with a positive message some time today.

2. Remember how you feel when people give you positive messages. Write down one of the positive messages you receive during the next week. Be sure to describe the situation.

Social Growth Program

Module Four: Warm Messages
For My Parents and Teachers

Child's Name _____

Group Leaders' Names _____

Today's Date _____

    Today's session reviewed how the messages we give each other affect our feelings. In particular, the children learned the distinction between positive, warm messages and negative, cold messages. Positive messages are communications that make us feel good and negative messages are communications that make us feel lousy. Positive messages include things like compliments, hugs, and words of encouragement. Negative messages are angry remarks, severe criticism, and nonresponsiveness.

    We practiced giving and receiving messages during a game. The children each received a bag with warm message tokens and cold message tokens. They distributed their tokens to each other as they gave out different kinds of messages. During this game, the children received feedback and instructions on how different kinds of messages affect us, on how to give positive messages, and on how to receive positive and negative messages from others.

Additional Comments:

INDIVIDUAL SESSION

Preparation Ideas for the Individual Session

The concept of "warm" positive messages versus negative messages is most easily illustrated when the discussion is accompanied by tangible tokens. The therapist can prepare these tangible tokens or symbols for use during the session. Some positive tokens are cotton balls, construction paper shapes (stars, hearts, circles), or pieces of flannel. Some negative tokens could be small balls of aluminum foil, or pieces of sandpaper. Other than these tokens, no special materials or preparation are needed for the Warm Messages module.

Guidelines for Conducting the Individual Session

Introduction

The therapist can begin by pointing out that we all give and receive many kinds of messages. She might role-play or dramatize several examples of positive, negative, or neutral communications, elaborating on positive messages like "I like your haircut," "You are a good singer," "Would you like to come to my birthday party?" and on negative messages like "Isn't it time for you to go home?" "You're stupid," "I think you're ugly." The therapist can ask the child to describe how the person at the receiving end of each message might feel. The child is given a bag of positive and negative tokens and instructed to give the appropriate one to the therapist after each message.

Following this introduction, the therapist can guide the discussion toward the child's own life experiences:

> Did anyone say anything really nice or kind to you today or yesterday? When was that? How did it make you feel? Did anyone say something mean to you this week? What was going on? How did that message make you feel? Today we are going to practice giving and receiving messages in ways that help us to make and keep friends.

Modeling

The therapist can begin this section by engaging the child in a brainstorming activity, which might include generating a "positive" list of situations or events when one child could give another child a positive message. The child can then choose one situation to role-play with the therapist. First, the therapist serves as a role model for giving a positive message, passing a positive token to the child each time she delivers a positive message, and reinforcing the child's efforts at acknowledging the message. Then roles are reversed and receiving a positive message is role-modeled. It is important to give some specific positive feedback for the child's initial efforts at giving and receiving positive messages. Here the concept of successive approximations is helpful: perfect performance is not the goal; rather, the therapist encourages and reinforces small steps toward an increasingly competent performance. The discussion can also focus on the feelings evoked by different messages during the role-plays.

Social Growth Program

Module Four: Warm Messages
For My Parents

Child's Name _____

Leader's Name _____

Today's Date _____

    Today's session emphasized how the messages we give each

other affect our feelings. _____ learned the distinction between positive, warm messages and negative, cold messages. Positive messages are those that make us feel good, whereas negative messages usually make us feel lousy. Positive messages include compliments and words of encouragement. Negative messages might be angry remarks or severe criticism.

    We practiced giving and receiving positive messages. When we received a message that seemed positive or made us feel good about ourselves, we gave the message sender a positive token. This helped us to think carefully about the effect our messages have on others.

_____ may bring home and give out one or more positive message tokens this week.

Additional Comments:

MODULE FIVE:

Asking Questions

GOALS

❑ Introduce the importance of asking questions when confused or afraid

❑ Practice effective ways of asking questions

❑ Model and discuss how others are affected by the way children ask questions

---

RATIONALE

Module Five empowers children to ask questions when they are puzzled, afraid, or curious about something. Responses are usually given to children's questions, and these responses are helpful in many ways. For one thing, they may help reduce children's fears and anxieties in new situations. Young children are sometimes not given information about something new and they often do not ask for this information. They may actively resist a new situation without having accurate information, or they may "suffer in silence" in anticipation of a dreaded expectancy. By learning to ask for more information, children will have a more accurate representation of what's likely to happen. This will enable them to feel more in control of the situation and less helpless and afraid.

Asking questions also helps young children clarify tasks and expectations so that they can solve problems effectively and choose a good course of action. If a child does not ask, it is frequently assumed that he understands, but some children are too timid to let others know they are confused. For these children, asking questions will be a difficult social skill to learn, but it will prove extremely helpful to them in adjusting to changes and in succeeding in academic as well as social arenas.

GROUP SESSION

Preparation Ideas for the Group Session

Introduction

Kindergarten–Second Grade. The goal of the introduction is to help children understand *why* asking questions is important and what form a question takes. Group leaders might plan to use puppets or pantomimes to demonstrate how *not* asking questions could result in misunderstanding a homework assignment or feeling very confused in a new situation. Group leaders might also plan to use a blackboard or bring a large tablet to the group meeting room to list reasons for asking questions, and children could participate in the brainstorming effort to make the list. The section on how questions are formed is largely guided by children's comments during the group session: children may either be asked to contribute ideas about new or confusing situations, or group leaders could bring in pictures of children in different situations that would serve as a springboard for discussion of questions that children might want to ask. It might also be helpful to write in capital letters WHY, WHAT, and HOW on the poster board.

Second–Fourth Grade. Puppets or pantomimes might also be used to demonstrate the importance of asking questions with these children. Second- through fourth-grade children can probably take an active part in brainstorming reasons for asking questions. This makes it especially important to have available either a blackboard or a large tablet.

Modeling Asking Questions

Kindergarten–Second Grade. Group leaders might prepare either to play a guessing game or to present riddles with missing information during the group session. Children could be instructed to ask questions and try to solve the riddle. Group leaders could also use puppets to model asking each other different questions. If this module is used for more than one group session, group leaders might also prepare in later sessions to demonstrate the appropriate way to ask questions (i.e., using polite language, raising a hand). Group leaders can use puppets to stress how the way we ask questions affects others' responses to them. Stress the difference between a nicely asked question and a rudely, impatiently asked question.

Second–Fourth Grade. Group leaders might try developing a game, riddle, or situation where information is missing and the children will have to ask appropriate questions to solve the problem. If group leaders have an opportunity to spend additional time on this module, they might prepare to model different ways children can ask questions in the classroom, with parents, or with friends. Group leaders might prepare skits or pantomimes to demonstrate right ways versus wrong ways of asking questions. You might also prepare to point out the effect that the way questions are asked can have on the kinds of responses that others give.

Guidelines for Conducting the Group Session

Introduction

The module might be introduced in this way:

A social skill that helps us feel comfortable and get along well with others is *asking questions*. When we ask questions, we are seeking more information. This helps us to understand what is being said or requested of us. When we understand what's happening, we can make good decisions and avoid making mistakes.

Asking questions not only helps us understand what is expected of us and make decisions, it also helps us learn things we don't know about new or different situations. The more we know about changes that are occurring in our lives, the less nervous we feel when they happen. Let's consider a couple of examples. One might be a new school year beginning. I imagine this creates feelings of excitement as well as nervousness for many of you. Have any of you found that it helps to ask questions and find out your new teacher's name and what kids or friends are going to be in your classroom? Another example might be a child whose parent has to go to the hospital for some medical tests or an operation. This would be a scary situation for almost all children. It probably would help if the child asked questions and found out where the parent was going to be, how long the parent thought he or she would be there, and what kinds of things were going to go on in the hospital.

Asking questions can also be helpful when you are carrying on a conversation with someone. This lets the other person know that you are listening and are interested in what they are saying. Just as there are nice ways of talking to others, there are nice ways of asking questions. How you ask a question takes as much skill as knowing what to ask. It is helpful to show respect and not be angry or sarcastic when you are asking for information. When people are asked in anger, they tend to respond in an angry way that is not very helpful.

Modeling

1. Modeling Between Group Leaders.   During the first session, group leaders can model appropriate ways to ask questions in new or confusing situations. Here is an example of a skit that could be used with young children:

The Dentist

MOM: Molly, today I am taking you to our dentist to have your teeth checked.

MOLLY: Who is a dentist?

MOM: A dentist is a person who takes care of people's teeth.

MOLLY: Does it hurt?

MOM: Sometimes a little bit, but the dentist tries to be gentle.

MOLLY: What does his place look like?

MOM: A dentist has a bright, clean room with a big comfortable chair for her patients. There's a big light that she can pull down to get a better look at your teeth and gums. The dentist will talk to you and tell you what she's going to do and why. She will teach you the proper way to brush and care for your teeth. She will ask you to come back for regular check-ups.

MOLLY: Yeah, Mom, what time is my appointment?

A discussion of effective and ineffective ways to ask questions is recommended for the second or third session spent on Module Four. During this session, group leaders might also model ineffective ways of asking questions. As an example, one group leader might say, "I want you to come home right after school." The other group leader responds in a demanding, whiny voice, "How come you never let me play with my friends after school? You never let me do anything after school." This exaggerated role-play will help the children's efforts to identify ineffective ways of asking questions. The children might discuss how the mother might respond when she is asked, "How come . . .?" in such a way. Based on the children's feedback, the group leaders might model the same situation again, incorporating any suggestions. These suggestions usually include the importance of trying to be polite and using "I" statements (e.g., "I don't like it that I have to go home right after school. I feel left out of what the other kids are doing."). Group leaders should praise each child for their contributions to the group discussion.

2. Modeling Between Group Leaders and Children.   Group leaders can complete similar role-plays with each child, with group leader–child pairs taking turns asking and answering questions. Possible situations for role-plays include: Why did you take my book without asking? How do I make a cake for the party tomorrow? What will happen when you take me to the doctor's office? Verbal praise or other clear indicators of success, such as circles or stars cut from construction paper, can be used. If these have been described as prizes for social skills successes, they will have meaning for most children. Reinforcers do not need to have monetary value to serve as recognition of effort, and improvement can be a powerful consequence in and of itself.

3. Modeling Between Children.   Group leaders might begin this portion of the session by asking children to brainstorm possible confusing situations, which could be listed on a large tablet for all the children to see. Then children could pair up and take turns asking and answering questions in these situations.

Discussion

With the children's help, group leaders can review the importance of asking questions when more information is needed. During the second group session devoted to this module, the children's FOR ME assignments can also be reviewed. These "real-life" examples will often have more meaning for the children than examples generated by group leaders. The group can also review how the way a question is asked affects others.

Social Growth Program

Module Five: Asking Questions
For Me

1. Write down one situation when you asked a question to get more information this week. Keep track of the question or questions you asked and the response that you received. (*Example:* My father was doing a card trick. I asked him if he would teach me how to do the trick. "Dad, will you show me how to do that?" He taught me the trick, and I practiced for a while.)

2. Write a paragraph describing a situation when you would want to ask questions (that is, if you were lost in a store, confused by a homework assignment). Be prepared to present your situation during the next session so that other group members can practice asking questions in that situation.

Social Growth Program

Module Five: Asking Questions
For My Parents and Teachers

Child's Name _____

Group Leaders' Names _____

Today's Date _____

    Today's session introduced children to the importance of asking questions when they are puzzled, afraid, or need more information to solve a problem. By asking questions, children can clarify what is expected of them, solve problems, make decisions, and learn about new experiences or situations that make them afraid. When children fail to ask for more information, they may feel very uncomfortable in new situations, may not follow directions well, or may misunderstand problems or homework assignments.

    Children will also practice how to form a question properly and present it in a way that will help them get the information they need. The way children ask for more information can affect whether or not they receive a helpful answer. The children will practice asking questions in a variety of situations, with teachers, parents, and friends.

Additional Comments:

INDIVIDUAL SESSION

Preparation Ideas for the Individual Session

Preparation for individual sessions on Asking Questions primarily involves obtaining materials such as puppets and giving some thought to possible skits and role-plays. The therapist should also make a tentative plan about the number of sessions available for this module, a factor that will have an impact on reasonable goals as well as the pacing of a session.

During the introduction of this module, a puppet might help illustrate what happens when children do and do not ask questions in new and confusing situations. This requires some advance thinking, but it is a good lead into a discussion of confusing situations that the child has actually faced. The puppet might also be used to demonstrate good ways to ask questions. Perfect models are not necessarily most helpful when teaching young children; portrayal of some struggles or mistakes as well as how to overcome them is often more beneficial. Finally, the therapist should plan to have some writing materials available, particularly for older children.

Guidelines for Conducting the Individual Session

Introducing Asking Questions

The importance of asking questions when a child is confused, afraid, or perhaps only curious can be illustrated in a number of ways. The therapist might begin by describing or dramatizing some common situations. Depending on the child's age and usual activities, these situations could include: confusing homework assignment, moving truck next door, upcoming trip to dentist, first night away from home, conversation with a new friend. Following each illustration, the child can be encouraged to explain how asking a question did or could have helped. The therapist can facilitate a discussion of how questions help us gather information, better understand what's going on and what's expected of us, and feel more comfortable with new experiences.

Modeling Asking Questions

During an individual session, the therapist can use the same situations as group leaders do to model appropriate and inappropriate ways of asking questions. The child can work with the therapist to label what distinguishes the obviously appropriate from inappropriate dramatizations. Some children who particularly enjoy playacting or "being on stage" might enjoy taking turns with the therapist in putting on a brief puppet show or role play. Other children might involve themselves by offering possible situations for dramatization. With older children, it's also possible to write out questions on paper. The therapist should be sure to discuss the content of the question as well as the tone used in asking questions. Verbal and nonverbal aspects of communication affect others' responses and willingness to provide helpful answers.

Social Growth Program

Module Five: Asking Questions
For My Parents

Child's Name _____

Leader's Name _____

Today's Date _____

    Today's session introduced _____ to the importance of asking questions when puzzled, afraid, or in need of more information to solve a problem. By asking questions, children can clarify what is expected of them, solve problems, make better decisions, and learn about new experiences or situations that make them afraid. When children fail to ask for more information, they may feel very uncomfortable in new situations, may not follow directions well, or may misunderstand problems or homework assignments.

    We will be practicing how to ask questions in an appropriate way. The way children ask for more information can affect whether or not they receive a helpful answer.

Additional Comments:

MODULE SIX:

Sharing Feelings

GOALS

- ❏ Introduce children to the importance of feelings in social exchanges
- ❏ Help children discriminate and label feelings or emotions in others
- ❏ Teach children how they can respond to others using empathy

---

RATIONALE

Module Six teaches the understanding and accurate labeling of feelings or emotions in others. Empathy is the ability to relate accurately and honestly to another person's feelings and emotions. To be truly empathic, one must be able to recognize emotions in another, see the emotional situation from another's perspective, and experience or share the positive or negative emotion.

Many believe that empathy is an important part of healthy social relationships. By understanding what someone else is experiencing, a child can respond appropriately in social situations. Also, by being able to share feelings with other people, we let them know that we are listening to what they are saying; we convey that we are understanding, concerned, and respectful. This sharing of feelings or emotional experiences is a vital part of forming close friendships. By learning to communicate empathy, some children can reduce their social isolation and improve their friendships. Most children respond positively when they feel that someone is trying to understand how they feel and cares about how they are feeling.

GROUP SESSION

Preparation Ideas for the Group Session

Introduction

The preparation for this module is similar for kindergarten children through fourth-graders. Group leaders might collect pictures, clipped from newspapers and magazines, of people expressing a wide range of emotions (e.g., happy, sad, surprised, angry). These pictures will be useful in helping children discriminate and label emotions in others. Alternatively, a chart could be prepared that lists various feelings. (Perhaps with the children's help, this chart could be completed during the group session.) Finally, group leaders might generate stories in which characters experience emotion-evoking situations. Newspapers or magazines could be one source of such story material, but group leaders should feel free to make up their own stories. These stories should be very brief. Here is an example:

Bob's Birthday

Bob said, "It was my birthday. When I came home from my paper route, all the lights were out in the house. When I turned them on, I saw all my friends and family in the living room. They all shouted, 'Happy Birthday.' I couldn't believe it."

Modeling Empathic Responses

Group leaders can prepare for the modeling section of the session by familiarizing themselves with the "empathy scenes" prior to the group session, two examples of which are included under "Guidelines for the Group Session." These scenes portray a child who has lost his dog and a child who's going to take a trip in an airplane. Each scene is written so that it can be modeled with positive and empathic as well as negative and nonempathic responses to illustrate how these types of responses affect social relationships. Group leaders may want to design some of their own scenes as well.

Guidelines for Conducting the Group Session

Introduction

The module might be introduced in two parts:

What's Empathy?   Group leaders say:

Today we are going to talk about feelings. We are also going to talk about sharing. Now we won't be talking about sharing candy or sharing toys. We're going to be talking about sharing feelings. What do we mean by sharing feelings? Well, if a friend of yours is feeling sad or maybe even crying, do you ever feel sad? [*Ask for specific instances.*] If another boy or girl is really happy about something, do you ever feel happy, too? [*Once again, ask for specific instances.*] If your mom gets really excited about good news, do you get excited? This is what we mean by sharing feelings and this sharing is called *empathy*. Empathy means understanding how a person is feeling or thinking and letting them know that you feel like they do.

Why Is It Good to Share Feelings?   Group leaders say:

Well, the other person often feels good because he or she knows that you understand how they are feeling and that you care. Empathy is also good for you. You might feel good because you helped another person. Also you might find that you make friends or improve friendships when you share feelings.

How Can You Find Out How Others Are Feeling?   Group leaders say:

Today we are going to learn how to share feelings. The first thing we have to learn is how to find out how others are feeling. One way is to watch them. [*Refer to the magazine or newspaper pictures that depict people expressing different emotions. Work with the children to identify what emotion is being expressed and how they can tell.*] Have you ever felt this way? If this person was your friend, how would you feel?

Another way to find out how others are feeling is to listen to what they say. [*Read stories, such as "Bob's Birthday," that evoke specific emotions.*] How do you think Bob was feeling? How would you have felt if Bob was your friend?

We have talked about ways to know how somebody else is feeling. We can watch them and we can listen to them, but how can you share these feelings with them so that they will know you understand and care for them? Now we are going to turn to modeling how we can share these feelings.

Modeling Empathic Responses

1. Modeling Between Group Leaders. Now group leaders tell the group:

We are going to show you some ways to share feelings or to express empathy for someone else. First, we will do it, then we will give you a chance.

Group leaders will now model each of the following scenes twice, using the positive (empathic) response first and the negative (nonempathic) response second:

Scene 1

ACTOR 1: [*Sits with head in hands looking sad.*]

ACTOR 2: What's the matter, [*name*]? Did something happen?

ACTOR 1: Yes, my dog Skippy ran away, and I can't find him anywhere.

Positive Response

ACTOR 2: Boy, I feel sad about that. Is there anything I can do to help?

ACTOR 1: Well, maybe we can go out together and look for Skippy. I didn't think anybody cared.

Negative Response

ACTOR 2: Oh well, there are lots of dogs in the world. Cheer up.

ACTOR 1: Oh, just leave me alone.

Scene 2

ACTOR 1: [*Runs up to Actor 2.*] Guess what? I just found out that I'm going to take a trip in an airplane to New York City.

Positive Response

ACTOR 2: Wow, that's fantastic. I'm really excited for you.

ACTOR 1: Thanks, I'll be sure to send you a postcard.

Negative Response

ACTOR 2: So what? I've been in an airplane a hundred times.

ACTOR 1: Oh, really. See you later.

2. Modeling Between Group Leader and Child.   The group leader might be Actor 1 and each child could be Actor 2 in one of the scenes or skits. Kindergarten and first-grade children will need to be coached and helped with their responses. For these younger children, acting out each scene and identifying the feelings is a reasonable expectation. Group leaders should try to run through each scene twice. Older children can be helped to respond in a way that will share feelings in one skit (positive or empathic response) and in a way that will not share feelings in another skit (negative or nonempathic response). It is important to discuss how Actor 1 would feel in each of the scenes.

Possible Scenes

1. Actor 1 feels angry because her math paper was torn up by a classmate.

2. Actor 1 feels sad because he has a sick grandmother.

3. Actor 1 feels proud because she has taught her puppy a new trick.

4. Actor 1 feels scared because he is lost in the shopping mall.

3. Modeling Between Children.   This activity is optional, depending on how well the children have responded to the previous activities. Also, these skits, with children playing both roles, may only be useful with the older children. It helps to provide the child who takes the part of Actor 1 with a first line. Group leaders should instruct the child who takes the part of Actor 2 to respond in a way that either shares or does not share feelings. After each skit, group leaders should ask the child to share how he or she felt with the group.

Possible Scenes

1.   Actor 1 is sad because his best friend just moved away.

2.   Actor 1 is a young child who's crying outside a store because he can't find his father.

4. Group Discussion.   Discuss with the children whether or not they would feel closer to someone who shares feelings with them. Why is it good to share feelings? How do you feel when someone is happy? When you are happy or sad, do you ever share these feelings with friends? Be sure and leave some time to review the FOR ME homework assignment.

Social Growth Program

Module Six: Sharing Feelings
For Me

1. Find and clip four pictures from newspapers or magazines that display people expressing different feelings. Bring these to the next group session.

2. Try to share feelings with someone in your family or one of your friends in the next few days. Let the group leader know what you did and what happened.

3. Remember that friends share feelings. Let a good friend know that you are feeling happy or sad so that they can share the feeling with you.

Social Growth Program

Module Six: Sharing Feelings
For My Parents and Teachers

Child's Name ⎯⎯⎯⎯⎯⎯⎯⎯⎯⎯⎯⎯⎯⎯⎯⎯⎯⎯⎯⎯⎯⎯⎯⎯

Group Leaders' Names ⎯⎯⎯⎯⎯⎯⎯⎯⎯⎯⎯⎯⎯⎯⎯⎯⎯⎯⎯⎯

Today's Date ⎯⎯⎯⎯⎯⎯⎯⎯⎯⎯⎯⎯⎯⎯⎯⎯

Today's session centered on how empathy, or understanding and sharing the feelings of another, is important in getting along with others. The children began learning how to tell how another person is feeling. They also learned how to share those feelings.

The children looked at pictures of people involved in different activities and tried to identify their feelings or emotions from facial expressions. They also listened to brief stories and identified the feelings of each person in the story. The children then played a game in which they practiced identifying and sharing feelings with group leaders and other children. Finally, they discussed how sharing feelings with another could help both people feel better and could help in making friends.

Additional Comments:

INDIVIDUAL SESSION

Preparation Ideas for the Individual Session

Introducing Sharing Feelings

The therapist can prepare for this session by gathering materials, such as magazine pictures, that can be used to illustrate a wide range of feelings or emotions. Short, thumbnail stories that illustrate different feelings are also helpful. If it proves difficult to find any such stories, the therapist may want to make up three or four that will have meaning for the child with whom you are working. An example is "Bob's Birthday," given in the preparation ideas for the group session.

Modeling Empathic Responses

The modeling of empathic responses can be done in one of two ways during individual sessions. The therapist who enjoys acting might choose to act out the "empathy scenes" included in the previous section on group sessions. This would require the therapist to play two parts (or use two puppets) and also to familiarize himself with these scenes before the individual session. Those therapists whose preferences lean more toward storytelling than acting might use illustrated stories to show children different kinds of responses to others' feelings. This will require some browsing at the neighborhood library, but many good possibilities are available.

Guidelines for Conducting the Individual Session

Introduction

The module might be introduced in this way:

Today we are going to talk about our feelings and other people's feelings. Let's think of times when we have felt happy . . . sad . . . angry . . . excited . . . scared. If we think about it, we can usually figure out how we are feeling. What about other people? Can we find out how others are feeling? Let's look at some pictures. [*Bring out magazine or storybook pictures.*] One way to tell how others are feeling is to look at their expressions. [*Help the child identify different emotions.*] How else can we tell what others are feeling? We could listen to what they say. Let's listen carefully to this story. [*Read short stories and help child identify emotions.*]

How might it help us to know what someone else is feeling? Do you sometimes notice how your friend . . . mother . . . brother is feeling? It helps us to know because then we can share our feelings. Empathy is sharing feelings. It means understanding how a person is feeling and letting that person know you care. It helps others feel understood and cared for. Empathy is important in building good friendships.

Modeling Empathic Responses

The therapist might begin by saying, "Let's learn some ways to share feelings or express empathy for someone else." Depending on personal preference, the therapist might then act out "empathy scenes" with positive (empathic) responses and negative (nonempathic) responses. Another option is to read short stories that illustrate these same responses. After a few examples, the child can be encouraged to label responses as "good" (empathic) or "bad" (nonempathic). If the therapist is using "empathy scenes" or skits, some children might be eager and willing to take part, too.

Social Growth Program

Module Six: Sharing Feelings
For My Parent

Child's Name _____

Leader's Name _____

Today's Date _____

    Today's session focused on feelings. We talked about how empathy, or understanding and sharing the feelings of another, is

important in getting along with others. _____
learned how empathy is important in forming and keeping good friendships. We also practiced figuring out how other people are feeling by watching them and listening to them. We looked at pictures of people and identified the feelings or emotions expressed.

Finally, we played a game in which _____

Additional Comments:

MODULE SEVEN:

Standing Up for Me

GOALS

- ❏ To help children understand their personal rights to be safe, voice some complaints, and refuse some requests
- ❏ To teach children how to express their personal rights

RATIONALE

Module Seven helps children understand what their rights are and how they can express them. It focuses on children's rights *to be safe, voice some complaints,* and *refuse some requests*. The expression of these three rights will help children protect themselves and feel good about themselves as individuals.

All of us have a right to feel safe and not be intimidated or threatened. Children sometimes need to refuse requests or resist situations that are harmful. They need to express their concerns persistently to trusted adults. Many times children are not taught to say *no,* when to say it, or how to say it. In "Standing Up for Me", children will practice saying *no* in situations that may be harmful. They will practice saying *no* in ways that are not hurtful to others.

Children have a right to have some of their opinions heard. This includes the opportunity sometimes to refuse requests or to voice dissatisfaction. Doing this requires tact, timing, and an ability to verbalize concerns constructively. This module will teach children to make complaints without whining or irritating others. The purpose of expressing ourselves, especially when making complaints, is to correct a problem situation that is bothering us. This expression is not used to hurt others but rather to make a situation better.

GROUP SESSION

Preparation Ideas for the Group Session

Introduction: Understanding Personal Rights

This module was designed for use in a minimum of three group sessions. The preparation is similar for kindergarten through fourth-grade children. Some visual aids will be helpful as group leaders introduce children to their personal rights. With this in mind, the following three posters are recommended:

---

1. MY RIGHTS

Feel safe

Refuse some requests

Voice some complaints

---

2. WHY RIGHTS ARE IMPORTANT!

Protect ourselves

Feel good about ourselves

---

3. FOUR STEPS TO SAFETY*

Know when you don't feel safe

Speak out when you're afraid

Name four adults you trust

Speak out until you feel safe again

---

*Adapted from Protective Behaviors (1984), *Safe, adventurous and loving* (Madison, WI: Protective Behaviors, Inc.).

Modeling the Expression of Personal Rights

The preparation of some props, such as paper microphones or cardboard masks, might make it easier for some children, especially kindergarten and first-grade children, to speak up in a group. Depending on the length of the session and the extent to which the group leaders can bring in precut materials, it might be possible to involve children in making, or at least finishing, these props. An alternative appropriate for all ages is puppets.

Group leaders might also prepare either by familiarizing themselves with the suggested role-play situations included under "Guidelines for Conducting the Group Session" or by designing some of their own situations for use during the session.

GUIDELINES FOR CONDUCTING THE GROUP SESSION

Session 1

Introduction

The module might be introduced in this way:

> During the next couple of sessions, we are going to discuss our personal rights and how we can speak up for these rights. By this, we mean letting other people know how we wish to be treated or letting them know they are doing something that is wrong and that we don't like. The three rights we will be discussing are the *right to feel safe*, the *right to refuse some requests*, and the *right to voice some complaints*.
>
> Why is speaking up for our rights important? Speaking up for our rights helps us to protect ourselves and feel good about ourselves. We let others know how we want to be treated. Speaking up for our rights does not mean we should try to hurt others, but it does mean that we should try to make things better. As we practice speaking up for our rights, it will help to try to remember what we have learned in previous group sessions. In particular, what we have learned about active listening, giving warm messages, and considering others' feelings will be important.
>
> Today we will talk about the right to express ourselves. What do you think we mean by "expressing ourselves"? It could mean we tell people what we like or what we don't like. This might include voicing our opinions or making complaints. We express our likes and dislikes, not to hurt others, but to make things better. How we express ourselves is very important! We try to remember to stay calm when describing what we don't like. Although we may feel angry, we can express this anger without abusing others. Responses such as name-

calling could have a negative result because the person is more likely to refuse to listen to us.

Modeling

1. Modeling Between Group Leaders. The group leader might say:

All of us have been in situations (or have had things happen to us) when we would have liked to express our dislikes or unhappiness, but did not.

Group leaders then model an example of an appropriate way to express yourself in such a situation. One possibility is the following scene:

MOTHER: Sally, what would you like me to pack in your lunch today?

SALLY: I don't care.

MOTHER: Would you like an egg salad sandwich?

SALLY: That's all right, I guess.

[*Later that afternoon*]

SALLY: Mom, how come you didn't pack a jelly sandwich in my lunch today?

MOTHER: Sally, remember this morning when I asked what you would like in your lunch? You could have suggested a jelly sandwich, I would have been happy to make you one.

SALLY: Okay, tomorrow I will tell you what I would like.

2. Modeling Between Group Leader and Children. Help the children list situations when they would have liked to express dissatisfaction but did not know how to or were afraid of the consequences. If they need help getting started with this brainstorming activity, possible situations to discuss might include: someone cutting in line in front of them, being bullied, someone taking their turn out of turn, or someone refusing to share with them. The role-play between group leader and child will be easier for the child if the group leader begins by writing out the parts on a large tablet. Choose several of the children's ideas and write out parts to brief role-plays. Then choose two of these and role-play them with each of the children in the group.

3. Modeling Between Children. Each of the children in the group should be given an opportunity to choose one of the situations on the tablet. A child might be invited to choose one they have already role-played with a group leader or one of the other situations. Two children then take turns in the role-play. The group leaders are there to facilitate the role-play and offer positive feedback to the children for their efforts.

4. Group Discussion.   Group leaders can guide children in a review of their personal rights. A discussion of how we express our opinions effectively can include examples from the role-plays enacted during the session. This will also offer a good opportunity to tie in material on active listening and empathy from previous sessions. Be sure and review the FOR ME and FOR MY PARENTS AND TEACHERS papers.

Session 2

Introduction

The group leader might begin by saying:

Last time we talked about the right way to voice our opinions and make some complaints. Another right that we have is the right to *refuse some requests.* By this we mean the right to say *no* when somebody asks you to do something, especially something we know we should not do. What would be an example of someone asking you to do something you shouldn't do? [*Cheating on homework, disobeying a class or home rule.*] What do we mean by saying *no* nicely? It means without intentionally hurting the other person's feelings. This is what we mean by being polite.

Modeling

1. Modeling Between Group Leaders.   The group leader might say, "Let's talk about times when you wanted to say *no* but didn't." Group leaders give an example and role-play the situation. As in the previous session, group leaders should engage the children in a brainstorming activity and have them list situations when they would want to say *no* even though it might be difficult. During this activity, it might be useful to incorporate harmful situations such as throwing rocks at cars or smoking behind the garage, as in the following example:

Refusing a Request
> EVA: Say, Mary, I found some cigarettes in my dad's car. Let's go behind the garage and smoke.
>
> MARY: Oh, I don't think I want to.
>
> EVA: Oh, come on. The gang will be there, Sally, Tom, Jim, the whole bunch.
>
> MARY: We'll probably get sick doing it. People that smoke smell like cigarettes, so our folks will find out what we did. We aren't supposed to be playing with matches and we might get the garage on fire.

EVA: Come on, you don't want to have any fun or do anything different.

MARY: Sorry, Eva. I think it is wrong and I'm not going to do it.

2. Between Group Leaders and Children.   Group leaders should refer back to the list of situations the children helped generate and choose one situation from the list to role-play with each child. They should try to model or practice appropriate as well as inappropriate ways to refuse a request. After each role-play, it is important to offer the child constructive feedback and praise them for their positive efforts.

3. Modeling Between Children.   Each child can be invited to choose one of the situations from the list, which the child will then role-play with another child. Group leaders might want to put the name of each child into a hat or box so that the child's partner for the role-play can be drawn at random. The group leader can facilitate the role-play and offer positive feedback to each of the participants.

4. Group Discussion.   The group discussion is an opportunity to review children's personal rights and discuss what the children learned about saying *no* and refusing requests. Group leaders should review the FOR ME homework assignment during the discussion.

Session 3

Introduction

This session might be introduced in this way:

> During the last two sessions, we discussed what our personal rights are and what it means to stand up for our rights. We learned how to voice complaints and refuse requests. Today we are going to discuss the right to feel safe all the time.
>
> What does "feeling safe" feel like to you? It may be a warm, comfortable feeling or a strong, confident feeling. What would it feel like to you? What does it feel like not to be safe? It might be that your heart beats real fast or your stomach feels funny. What does it feel like to you?
>
> What should we do when we feel unsafe? During our session today we will talk about what we can do. We will talk about how we can share our feeling with someone we trust. We will each list at least four adults with whom we can share things. If we are feeling unsafe, we will learn that we need to tell these people and keep telling them until we feel safe.

Group Activities

Group leaders should help children identify how they know when they are feeling safe or feeling unsafe. It might help to make a list of the children's responses under two headings, "Feeling Safe" and "Feeling Unsafe." This should be done as a brainstorming activity so that all of the children's responses are accepted without judgment.

As a second activity, the children can be invited to brainstorm a list of situations when they might feel unsafe. If they need help in getting the list started, some ideas might include noises in the night, being lost in a store, or seeing a stranger at the door when home alone. Each child might be encouraged to name at least one situation in which he or she can recall having felt unsafe.

As a final group activity, group leaders should discuss with the children the importance of considering which adults they can trust. Children might be assisted to list the names of these adults, or this can be done with parents as a homework assignment. As a group activity, children might draw their network of trusted adults.

Social Growth Program

Module Seven: Standing Up for Me
For Me

Session 1

1. Write down at least two things that bothered you and that you could have complained about this week. Did you express your opinion or complain? If yes, how did you express yourself? If no, how might you have expressed yourself?

2. Recall a time when a friend or family member complained during the past week. How did that person complain? Write down the situation and share it during the next group session.

Session 2

3. Did you turn down any requests this week? Did you agree, say *yes,* to anything that you regret? Did you answer the way you really wanted to? Is it sometimes hard to answer the way you want to?

Session 3

4. Try to think of at least one situation at home or at school when you either stood up for your personal rights or wished that you had done this. What happened? What might you do differently next time?

5. Work with one of your parents to draw your own network of trusted, helpful adults to turn to when afraid.

Social Growth Program

Module Seven: Standing Up for Me
For My Parents and Teachers

Child's Name _____

Group Leaders' Names _____

Today's Date _____

Today's session was the first session in our unit on helping children understand and express their personal rights. We began talking about *ways to feel safe, voice some complaints,* and *refuse certain requests.* The expression of these rights helps children protect themselves, feel strong, and feel good about themselves.

The purpose of children's expressing themselves is to correct something that is bothering them. This expression of opinions or complaints is used to make things better rather than to hurt others. Children will practice making complaints without whining or irritating others. They will also learn when it is okay to refuse requests, and they will practice saying *no* to inappropriate requests. Finally, children will learn to identify when they feel afraid as well as what they can do about it. Children can learn the importance of trusting their feelings and speaking out to trusted adults when they feel afraid.

We will talk about identifying a network of four or more trusted adults. You might want to help your child draw up a personal network of people to turn to when he or she is afraid.

Additional Comments:

INDIVIDUAL SESSION

Preparation Ideas for the Individual Session

Introduction

The therapist might prepare one or two handouts, titled "My Rights" and "Four Steps to Safety," that can serve as visual aids during the session and memory aids after the session (see the preparation ideas for the group session). These handouts should parallel the posters recommended for the group session.

Modeling

Depending on the child's age, it might be appropriate to bring materials to the session that could be used in making paper microphones or some other type of "public speaking" prop. It will be very hard for some children to speak up for themselves, and props can provide a bridge to role-playing or play acting.

Guidelines for Conducting the Individual Session

This module could be the basis for several sessions and will probably require a minimum of three sessions. The therapist will want to decide, at least tentatively, whether or not the child would benefit from sessions spent on each of the rights covered in the module. This decision will enable the therapist to structure the introduction accordingly.

Session 1

Introduction

The therapist might introduce the session in this way:

> During the next couple of sessions, we are going to discuss our personal rights and how we can speak up for these rights. By this, we mean letting other people know how we wish to be treated or letting them know they are doing something that is wrong and that we don't like. Our rights include the *right to feel safe*, the *right to refuse some requests*, and the *right to voice some complaints*.
>
> Why is speaking up for our rights important? [*The therapist then listens to the child's thoughts and feelings about personal rights. During the ensuing discussion, the therapist conveys the following two messages:*] (1) Speaking up for our rights helps us to protect ourselves and feel good about ourselves, and (2) speaking up for our rights does not mean we should try to hurt others, but it does mean that we should try to make things better.

Let's start with our right to express ourselves. What do you think we mean by "expressing ourselves"? [*The therapist listens to the child's ideas and facilitates a discussion before continuing.*] It could mean we tell people what we like or what we don't like. This might include voicing our opinions or making complaints. We express our likes and dislikes, not to hurt others, but to make things better. How we express ourselves is very important! We try to remember to stay calm when describing what we don't like. This is sometimes difficult as we may feel very angry. Nevertheless, responses such as name calling could have a negative result because the person is more likely to refuse to listen to us.

Modeling

The therapist might introduce modeling in this way:

Let's begin by thinking of times or situations when you would have liked to express your dissatisfaction or unhappiness, but did not. How about during the last few days?

If the child needs help in considering possibilities, some probes or questions about student lunchroom behaviors, sibling intrusions, classroom bullies, or parent demands may orient the child. After identifying one or two recent situations, the therapist should ask the child why she did not express her opinion. (It will be important to acknowledge instances in which the child chooses not to express herself after carefully considering the consequences, as in choosing not to swear at or argue with a parent over a distasteful but reasonable chore, or not to tattle on another child who has played a harmless prank on her, even though she feels angry about it.) The therapist might work with the child to generate a list of situations in which the child might want to express dislike or unhappiness. The therapist can then role-play appropriate ways to express such feelings.

Session 2

Introduction

This session might begin as follows:

Last time we talked about the right way to voice our opinions and make some complaints. Another right that we have is the right to *refuse some requests*. By this we mean the right to say no when somebody asks us to do something, especially something we know we should not do. What would be an example of someone asking you to do something you shouldn't do? [*Cheating on homework, disobeying a class or home rule.*] What do we mean by saying no nicely? It means without hurting or abusing the other person.

Modeling

Here the therapist might say, "Let's see if we can make a list of situations when we might want to say *no*." The therapist will need to facilitate this brainstorming activity, perhaps offering suggestions of some harmful situations (throwing icy snowballs at car windshields, riding bikes down the middle of the road), some frightening situations, and some otherwise inappropriate situations (stealing $5 from father's wallet, cheating on a social studies test).

Then the therapist can ask the child to pick one of the situations from the list. The therapist can role-play saying *no* and then give the child a turn. Therapist and child can continue this role-playing activity with other situations on the list.

Session 3

Introduction

The therapist begins this session by introducing the *right to feel safe* in a way that is sensitive to the individual child. She might help the child identify what "feeling safe" is like. Is it warm and comfortable? Strong and confident? How is it different from feeling afraid? The child can be helped to recall a time when he felt afraid. What was it like? Did his heart beat quickly? Stomach feel funny? Body feel sweaty? It might be useful to make two lists with the child, "Feeling Safe" and "Feeling Unsafe."

The therapist can help the child understand that no one feels safe all the time, but we need to know what to do if we are feeling unsafe. The remainder of this session will emphasize the importance of sharing our scared feelings with someone we trust.

Activity

The therapist can help the child record his own network of trusted adults to turn to when afraid. The child may want to draw this network on a piece of paper. Another possibility is to have the child begin the list during the session and finish it (complete with phone numbers) with a parent at home.

Social Growth Program

Module Seven: Standing Up for Me
For My Parents

Child's Name _____

Leader's Name _____

Today's Date _____

  Today's session was the first session in our unit on personal rights. We began discussing the *right to feel safe*, the *right to voice some complaints*, and the *right to refuse certain requests*. We discussed how the expression of these rights can help us protect ourselves, feel strong, and feel good about ourselves.

  _____ will be practicing expressing opinions and making complaints without whining or irritating others. We will discuss how the purpose of expressing ourselves is to correct something that is bothering us. _____ will learn that it is sometimes okay to refuse requests and will practice saying *no*.

  Finally, _____ will learn to identify when he feels afraid and what he can do about it. _____ will learn the importance of trusting feelings and speaking out to adults when he feels afraid. I will be working with your child to identify a network of four or more trusted, helping adults. You might want to help your child draw up a network of people to whom they can turn when feeling afraid.

Additional Comments:

MODULE EIGHT:

Self-Control

GOALS

❑ Discuss the importance of self-control when children are playing with others, working on school assignments, and carrying on conversations

❑ Practice techniques for improving self-control

RATIONALE

Self-control is the ability to regulate or change one's behavior in the absence of external control. Children need to exert increasing amounts of self-control as they grow from early childhood to adulthood. This helps them feel good about themselves, complete tasks, and get along with others. Children will learn one or two techniques for exercising self-control. These techniques, *self-talk* and *self-observation,* both involve setting self-control standards and monitoring performance. The information and exercises in this module rely much on the past work of one of the present authors, Dan Kirschenbaum, and his associates from the Social Skills Development Program (Kirschenbaum, Bane, Fowler, Klei, Kuykendohl, Marsh, & Pedro, 1976).

Kanfer and Karoly (1972; Karoly & Kanfer, 1982) divided the self-control process into a Commitment Phase and an Execution Phase. Before trying to change or control an aspect of behavior, a person must commit himself to the change. The reasons usually have to be very strong to produce a strong commitment. Support from others is also helpful. But if, for example, a child is praised or given lots of special attention simply for *saying* he will work at self-improving, he will be less likely actually to improve himself. Such rewards are most helpful when they follow real self-control behaviors rather than mere promises.

Within this theory of self-control, the Execution Phase might also be referred to as a behavior phase. If a child wanted to control his impulse to fight (to reduce the frequency of his fighting), he would first need to *decide (make a commitment) to change*. Then he would need to set a *standard or goal*, such as: "During each Social Growth group session, I will not yell at other kids." Then he will need to *gather information* about his yelling during each group. By spending 2 or 3 minutes talking with a group leader at the end of each session, he could *evaluate* his yelling behavior by comparing the information gathered ("I did start yelling at Susie once") with his standard (no yelling). He could then self-punish by, for example, allowing himself only one graham cracker at the next snack time. If he met his standard of no yelling, then he could self-reward by choosing for himself a favorite character sticker or getting an extra graham cracker.

This model specifies *commitment, standard setting, systematic information gathering, self-evaluation,* and *self-reward* or *self-punishment* as important processes in self-control. Generally, in designing ways to help children improve their self-control skills, it is very useful to help them improve their abilities to make clear commitments, set realistic or attainable goals, gather and then evaluate information about their behavior, and, finally, deliver to themselves (with a little help from their friends or group leaders, perhaps) appropriate consequences. It is of some interest to note that training children in their ability to set standards for themselves may be one of the most important and necessary of these self-control steps.

GROUP SESSION

Preparation Ideas for the Group Session

This module requires a minimum of one introductory session as well as two or three sessions for each of the self-control techniques, self-talk and self-observational training. If group leaders have only two or three sessions available for the entire module, it would be beneficial to choose only one of the self-control techniques to present, model, and practice.

Introducing the Importance of Self-Control

Puppets or play acting could be used to show the importance of self-control when trying to *resist temptations, tolerate unpleasant situations,* or *learn new skills.* The following three "self-control types" could be used as a basis for these skits (Kirschenbaum et al., 1976):

The Child Who Resists Temptation.   Sometimes it's very hard to resist something. Let's consider a child who is very hungry and waiting for dinner. He knows there are some fresh chocolate chip cookies in the cookie jar even though it's against the rules in his house to dig in just before dinner.

Another example might be a child who loves to run around frantically when excited. Just like our first child, who needs to learn to resist the cookie jar before dinner, this child must learn how to resist the temptation to run around when she is in a classroom.

The Child Who Tolerates Something Unpleasant.   Sometimes we must *tolerate something unpleasant to reach a positive goal.* Just as the cartoon hero might suffer greatly as he tries to save his endangered friend, children sometimes feel they have "to suffer" before reaching goals. This might include cleaning their room to earn an allowance, working extra hours to complete a science project on time, or enduring heat and tiredness to complete a running race on their school's field day.

The Child Who Tries to Learn a New Skill.   The self-improver might be a child who is *attempting to learn any skill* (e.g., reading, playing soccer, doing a cartwheel, playing a piano) largely on her own. If no adult is overseeing her work, the child must control her impulses to be distracted or give up as she practices these new skills. As an example, the child who "hates math" might be much better off if he learns how to tolerate his frustrated feelings so he can continue working at math during class and at home.

Modeling Self-Control Skills

Self-talk Skills.   In a session designed to present, model, and practice self-talk skills, tasks or activities will provide the medium for modeling self-control. Group leaders can prepare materials for age-appropriate tasks before the session. Possibilities for kindergarten through second-grade children might include simple puzzles, copying a series of letters, or an agreement to talk about something like "favorite toys" for a set amount of time. Possible tasks or activities for second- through fourth-grade children might include working on a mock school assignment; playing the "topic game," which involves sticking to one topic of conversation for a predetermined amount of time; or completing a slightly more difficult puzzle.

Self-Observation Training.   Devise a system for counting and recording the frequency of children's behaviors. The younger kindergarten through second-grade children will need simple systems and perhaps some additional help with recording behaviors. Possibilities include stickers on a wall chart, a bead bracelet, or a small notepad and pencil for tallying behaviors. It is important that some type of visual record is used so that group leaders and children can refer to efforts during each session. Some of the older second- through fourth-grade children will enjoy setting up their own charts for recording the frequency of behaviors.

Guidelines for Conducting the Group Session

Introduction

The session might be introduced in this way:

Self-control means managing our own behavior. This is some-times very important because there are no parents, teachers, or group leaders standing next to you to manage your behavior. And some-times, even if adults are nearby, you want to take care of yourself.

Let's talk about some times when self-control is important. First, let's consider times when it's very hard to resist something. [*Present the skit "The child who resists temptation," described in the preparation ideas.*] What might happen if a child does not resist the temptation to eat the chocolate chip cookies? What might happen if he does resist the temptation? What about the child who wants to run around the classroom? What might happen if she runs around the classroom? How will it be different if she stays in her seat and does her work? [*Present examples of "The child who tolerates something unpleasant" and "The child who learns a new skill" and discuss the advantages of self-control.*]

Modeling Self-Talk

The group leader might begin by saying:

Many people worry about talking to themselves—"Oops! I'm talking to myself! I must be going crazy!" But talking to yourself can be very useful. It can help you keep your attention focused on something you're working on.

Using a procedure developed by Meichenbaum and Goodman (1971), many "impulsive" children have learned how to become less im-pulsive, better at learning in school, and more creative. Self-talk includes the following elements:

1. Group leaders *select a task* that requires concentrated work over a short period of time. The first task selected should be one that children are good at performing (see Self-Talk Preparation Ideas).

2. One group leader *models useful self-talk* by completing the task (e.g., a simple puzzle) while talking to himself about the task definition, his approach to the task, his efforts to keep his attention focused, and coping statements that he uses to get himself back on task if needed. For example, in the Topic Game the group leader could model the following self-talk before beginning his discussion of the topic:

What should I remember? Oh, I'm to finish talking about what I started to talk about. Okay. Think before talking and remember not to switch. Look at the cue card (card with the words "STOP, LISTEN, LOOK, and THINK Before Answering" written on it) to remember how to talk with you.*

3. The *child* then performs the same task while talking to himself *out loud*. It may be a good idea to have children take turns completing short, time-limited tasks.

4. The Group leader then performs the task while *whispering* to himself. The child then performs the task while whispering to herself.

5. Finally, the child attempts the task while *talking to himself silently*. Again, children need to take turns completing time-limited tasks.

These steps could be repeated for different tasks (tasks that involve repetition and no talking, such as solving simple math problems or copying letters). The use of cue cards or other written instructions can be very helpful at first and these can be carried away from the session by the child. Self-talk homework assignments (e.g., trying these out in the classroom or at home) are crucial if the self-talk skills are to be most helpful in many situations. Also, the child could actually plot his progress on given tasks on graph paper. Graphing is an important way to learn about setting standards, evaluating one's progress, and self-rewarding . . . not to mention a little mathematical learning on the side.

Modeling Self-Observation

Since one of the key elements in self-control is information gathering (sometimes referred to as self-monitoring or self-observation), this is an important skill to develop. Self-observational skills can be developed in many ways. Here is an example:

1. Group leaders and children select target behaviors, such as laughing, crying, hand raising, saying nice things to other children, or talking to someone. During the first self-observation group session, the children can help observe and record the frequency with which one of the group leaders engages in the target behavior. During the following group session, group leaders might assist the children in choosing their own target behavior relevant to their personal social growth goals.

2. Some system of recording the frequency of the target behaviors needs to be devised (see the preparation ideas for ways in which these behaviors could be counted). Frequency information could then be charted on a simple graph:

---

*Adapted from P. C. Kendal and A. J. Finch (1976). A cognitive behavioral treatment for impulsivity: A case study, *Journal of Consulting and Clinical Psychology, 44,* 852–857.

Johnnie's Impulses to Yell

	Monday	Tuesday	Wednesday	Thursday	Friday
8					
7					
6					
5					
4					
3					
2					
1					

Younger children will need simpler systems and some help with recording the information. One way to make a system simple is to observe and evaluate target behaviors during short time periods. For example, a clock in the group room might be marked off in 10-minute or 15-minute sections: Johnnie would need to watch the clock and if, for example, he felt the impulse to yell (target behavior) during the first 15 minutes, he might put a sticker on a simple wall chart.

Group leaders will want to prompt or cue each child about when to record something; that is, prompt or cue them when the target behavior has been observed. Possible cues might be a cue card, a bell, or a verbal prompt that signals the child to record her behavior. These cues or prompts should be gradually eliminated so that the child becomes more and more responsible for her own progress.

Discussion

The closing discussion enables the group leaders to review progress, which might be as simple as counting stickers or studying a chart or bar graph. Make an effort to reward any progress toward goals with encouragement and praise. Each child can also be helped to consider the extent to which his standard is realistic. When a second session is spent on this module, group leaders should review the FOR ME assignment with the children.

Social Growth Program

Module Eight: Self-Control
For Me

1. Think about your own self-control skills. List two types of school situations when it is most difficult for you to maintain self-control.

    Examples are:
    Finishing a difficult math test
    Keeping cool when someone yells at you during recess
    Waiting in line for your turn

2. Choose one of the school situations that is difficult for you.

    Set your own *self-control standard*. You may want to get help from group leaders, teachers, or parents in setting a reasonable standard.

Social Growth Program

Module Eight: Self-Control
For My Parents and Teachers

Child's Name _____

Group Leaders' Names _____

Today's Date _____

     Children learn to exert more and more self-control as they grow up. This helps them to feel good about themselves and take care of themselves when adults are not nearby.

     Today's session introduced children to the importance of self-control when they are playing with others, working on school assignments, and carrying on conversations. We gave examples of three situations when we manage or control our own behavior. These were when we need to *resist temptations* (eating too many cookies before dinner or giggling and running around the classroom), *tolerate unpleasant situations* (playing a game with someone who yells or pushes, doing a difficult math task), and *learn new skills* (practicing a new skill without giving up or getting distracted).

     During our next session, we will practice some self-control skills. We will practice setting self-control standards or goals, charting our efforts at self-control, and rewarding ourselves when we do well. Each child will then begin working on self-control skills specific to his or her own needs.

Additional Comments:

INDIVIDUAL SESSION

Preparation Ideas for the Individual Session

Introducing the Importance of Self-Control

Individual sessions offer the therapist a greater opportunity than group leaders have to identify events from the child's own life that illustrate the importance of self-control. These might be personal difficulties with self-control or observed events involving siblings at home or other children on the school playground. If discussing personal experiences is difficult initially for the child, the therapist could use puppets, skits, or story examples (see the Preparation Ideas for the group session for possibilities).

Modeling Self-Control Skills

Before the session, the therapist will want to plan some possible activities or tasks that can provide the medium for modeling and practicing self-talk skills. Activities are chosen according to the individual child's developmental level and interests, and the therapist may want to have a few options and involve the child in choosing the first activity. Possibilities for young children include simple puzzles, alphabet tasks (e.g., copying the alphabet), building a design with blocks, or the "Topic Game" (a brief, one-topic conversation). Older children may also enjoy the "Topic Game" as well as easy mock school assignments, "mind teasers," or building a simple model.

As preparation for self-observation training, the therapist should plan to have some type of counting or recording materials on hand during the session. The possibilities are numerous, and it's likely that the therapist has appropriate materials, including stickers, beads, or a notepad and paper, readily available.

Guidelines for Conducting the Individual Session

Introducing the Importance of Self-Control

The therapist might say:

Self-control means managing our own behavior. This is sometimes very important because there are no parents or teachers standing nearby to manage your behavior. And often, even if parents or other adults are nearby, you want to take care of yourself. Let's think of some examples. [*The therapist begins a brainstorming activity with the child, perhaps with the challenge to cover the chalkboard or paper with examples.*] Have you ever found it's hard to resist something?

Have you ever been tempted to do something you knew wasn't right? [*The therapist offers some examples for the list and accepts each of the child's ideas without judging their value.*] How about times when you have had to tolerate frustration to finish some assignment or reach some goal? [*The therapist again facilitates the brainstorming activity.*] How about when you've tried to learn a new skill? Did you ever feel like giving up?

Self-Talk Skills

The therapist might begin by saying:

Many people worry about talking to themselves—"Oops! I'm talking to myself! I must be going crazy!" But talking to yourself can be very useful. It can help you keep your attention focused on something you want to do well and finish.

The therapist then offers the child two or three activity options (see the preparation ideas for the group session). The therapist models self-talk, which involves completing the task while talking to himself about the task requirements, how to approach the task, efforts to keep his attention focused, and coping statements that help him get himself back on task as needed. The child then is helped to complete the same, time-limited task while talking to himself out loud. This is followed by the therapist's modeling the task while whispering, after which the child does the same. Finally, the therapist models completion of the task while thinking silently.

Self-Observation Training

The therapist should select a target behavior with the child. As a starting point, this might be something, such as laughing or looking out the window, that is completely unrelated to the child's social growth goals. During their first self-observation session, the child can help observe and record the frequency with which he (or the therapist) displays the target behavior. After two or three practice examples, the therapist assists the child in choosing a target behavior pertinent to the child's personal social growth goals and then gathers information on the frequency of this behavior (see the Preparation Ideas for simple recording systems). It might be necessary to cue the child with a verbal prompt when the behavior occurs, thereby signaling the child to record the behavior. The therapist should gradually eliminate these cues so that the child becomes more responsible for his own progress and should reward any steps toward effective self-control with praise and encouragement. Information from the FOR ME assignment should be integrated during the second or third session.

Social Growth Program

Moduel Eight: Self-Control
For My Parents

Child's Name _____

Leader's Name _____

Today's Date _____

    Children learn to exert more and more self-control as they grow up. This helps them to feel good about themselves and take care of themselves when adults are not nearby.

    Today's session introduced _____ to the importance of self-control when playing with others, working on school assignments, and carrying on conversations. We talked about three types of situations when we manage or control our own behavior. These were when we need to *resist temptations* (eating too many cookies before dinner or giggling and running around the classroom), *tolerate unpleasant situations* (playing a game with someone who yells or pushes, doing a difficult math task), and *learn new skills* (practicing a new skill without giving up or getting distracted).
    During our next session, we will identify some situations when it

is difficult for _____ to maintain self-control. We will then begin practicing some self-control skills. We will practice setting self-control standards or goals, charting efforts at self-control, and rewarding successes.

Additional Comments:

MODULE NINE:

Social Problem Solving

GOALS

- ❏ Teach children to think of *alternatives*—"What else can I do?"—when confronted with interpersonal problems
- ❏ Teach children to think of the *consequences* of alternative responses
- ❏ Encourage children to choose the best alternative after considering various consequences

RATIONALE

Young children cannot completely avoid conflicts with brothers and sisters or friends and classmates. Some conflict is inevitable as children try to satisfy their own desires in the company of others. In effective social problem solving, children *think* about ways to respond when faced with these conflicts.

This module, which draws upon the work of Kirschenbaum and associates from the Social Skills Development Program (SSDP; 1976), will teach children social problem solving skills. Spivak and Shure (1974) have described one approach to teaching children how to solve interpersonal problems. Their program was designed to teach young children basic language concepts that are helpful in problem solving. An understanding of concepts such as "same–different," "might," and "why–because" is necessary in learning *alternative, consequential,* and *causal thinking*. What is most exciting about this approach is that research evaluations demonstrate that it can be helpful for children of a variety of ages from all socioeconomic and cultural groups.

GROUP SESSION

Preparation Ideas for the Group Session

During the introductory phase of this module, group leaders will want to make certain that children understand what is meant by social or interpersonal conflict. Group leaders might plan to have a blackboard, a large tablet, or a poster board available to record examples of social problems or conflicts that the children generate during this introductory discussion. We have also included a number of sample problem situations that could be used during this discussion or one of the later sections on developing alternative or consequential thinking. Group leaders might find it helpful to familiarize themselves with these sample situations before the group session:

Social Problem Situations

1. Mary and her older brother Jason are grocery shopping with their father. Mary wants Jason to give her a chance to push the grocery cart.

2. Four students are working on their art projects together at a work station. Benjamin wants Sarah to let him use the scissors, but she won't let him.

3. Michelle really wants her brother to look at her drawing, but he is watching television.

4. Tom and Michael are feeding the geese at the pond. Tom is holding the bag of corn. He doles out small handfuls to Michael. Michael wants a chance to "be in charge" of the feed.

5. Carol and Amanda were playing with splatter paint in Amanda's basement. Just as they are finishing a painting, Carol says she has to go home. Amanda thinks Carol should help her clean up the big mess.

6. John and Cameron are sledding together. They have borrowed John's older brother's sled. During one of their runs, a runner breaks off the sled. Cameron wants to just pretend it didn't happen, but John thinks they should tell his older brother together.

7. Mary wants to have a birthday slumber party. Her mother and father told her that she can invite no more than five girls to her slumber party. Mary doesn't know how she can possibly invite just five girls and not hurt anyone's feelings.

8. Jennifer has lots of new stickers that are all the same. She would like to trade some with a classmate but feels like she's been left out.

Guidelines for Conducting the Group Session

Introduction

The module might be introduced in this way:

> We have been practicing many skills that help us get along well with others. The skills of listening, giving positive messages, and empathy will help us to make friends, keep friends, and avoid some conflicts with others. Despite our very best efforts, though, some conflicts with others are bound to happen. This is because what we want and need, or what we think is right, will not always match what others want or need or think is right. When this happens, we need to resolve the conflict. Let's consider some conflicts with brothers and sisters or classmates and friends that you've experienced.

Group leaders record conflict situations on a blackboard, large tablet, or poster board. Be careful to do this without discussing or evaluating *how* the child handled the conflict. This will encourage children to contribute their experiences without fear of evaluation. If additional ideas are needed, some of the problem situations included under Preparation Ideas could be offered as examples. It would probably be helpful for one of the group leaders to restate the problems while recording them.

Developing Alternative Thinking

The group leader might say:

> We have seen that none of us can completely avoid conflicts with others. Today we will begin to learn how to solve these conflicts or problems by thinking of alternative, or different, solutions. We're going to play a game. The idea of this game is to think of lots of different ways to act or behave when we face different problems. We will talk about some of the problems we've listed here.

The group leaders begin by choosing, perhaps with the children's help, one of the problems from the list that has been generated. The group leaders write this problem clearly on a blackboard or tablet and repeat that the idea of the game is to think of lots of different ways of dealing with the problem. To motivate the children (even though the younger ones may not be able to read very well), group leaders tell them they are going to try to fill up the whole blackboard with the children's ideas as they tell them. Another possibility for older children is to have them jot down ideas on a large paper tablet or paper tablecloth; all the children can take part in trying to fill the paper. After a few ideas are given, it's helpful to count them out and talk about the ways that they are similar or different. Group leaders should encourage all relevant solutions, aggressive, forceful, or not; if a consequence of a solution is offered, they should not discourage it but continue asking for more solutions. Sometimes a child will say something that seems irrelevant to the problem, such as "Make him happy" as a way to get a chance to play with a desired toy. Ask the child, "How can you make him happy?" If a truly irrelevant solution is offered, ask, "Why is that a good idea?" It is important to be as accepting and noncritical as possible during this brainstorming activity.

If a solution is repeated, group leaders can identify it as a repetition by saying something like, "Well, that's just like when Heather said, 'Grab the jumprope away' [to the problem of one girl wanting to play with another girl's jumprope]. Do you have different ideas?" A solution might also be offered that is an elaboration of a previous solution. One solution given to the problem of two girls wanting to play with the same jumprope, for example, might be, "Offer her some candy for a chance to play." Other elaborations children might mention include: "Give her some ice cream," "Give her potato chips." When these repetitions or elaborations come up, it's important to help the children classify them as such. For instance, group leaders might comment, "Giving ice cream and candy and potato chips are all giving something. Can anyone think of an idea that's different from giving something?"

Developing Consequential Thinking

The group leader might say:

> We have all practiced thinking of more than one way to solve conflicts with others. Now let's think about the consequences or results of each of these solutions. What is a consequence? A consequence is an outcome of something that we do. It might be the reaction of a second person to something that we have done or said. For example, if Sam hits Sarah, Sarah might hit Sam back, tell Sam's mother, cry, walk away, or tell Sam that she didn't like that. We don't know exactly what will happen, but we can think about what *might happen*. Let's begin by choosing one of the problem situations for which we've identified many possible solutions.

It is helpful to choose a problem situation that is conducive to naming consequences. Sometimes a problem situation that involves something concrete like refusal to share is a good way to begin, because solutions such as hit, grab, ask, and tell someone are usually generated. One problem situation involving sharing might be as follows: Jason wants Sarah and Jennifer to give him a chance to play on the tire swing. The group leaders can list this situation on the board and request a solution. Let's assume that the first solution given is that Jason can ask Sarah and Jennifer for a chance to get on the tire swing. The group leader says: "Pretend Jason did ask for a chance, let's fill up the whole blackboard with ideas of what might happen next." Or: "How might Sarah or Jennifer feel if Jason asked them for a chance?" Or: "What might Sarah or Jennifer say if Jason asked them for a chance?" Or: "What might they do if Jason asked them for a chance?"

Using one solution at a time, elicit as many possible consequences as you can before going on to a new solution. It would be helpful to draw out a diagram like this one:

The group leaders can handle repetitions and elaborations in the same way that they used for the exercise on alternative thinking: by repeating and classifying elaborations and then asking for another consequence.

As group leaders work with the children to develop causal thinking (or solution-consequence pairing), they will need to add an additional step: consideration of the pros and cons of each solution to a given problem. This step might involve giving multiple solutions to a problem (such as Jason wanting Sarah and Jennifer to give him a chance to swing) and the possible consequences of each of these solutions. After eliciting each alternative solution, group leaders immediately ask the children for consequences. After they have given two or three consequences, group leaders go on to a second alternative solution. Finally, group leaders have the children decide which alternative is best. Let's consider an example.

Problem

Michelle wants Brittany to help her put away the board game.

GROUP LEADER: Can anyone think of one way that Michelle might try to get Brittany's help?

CHILD: She could ask Brittany.

GROUP LEADER: Good, what *might* happen if she asks Brittany to help her put away the board game?

CHILD: Brittany will help her.

GROUP LEADER: I'll write that on the board like this.

Ask Brittany	She'll help her

GROUP LEADER: [*Elicits another response*] Can anyone think of another thing that might happen if she asks Brittany?

CHILD: Brittany will say maybe I'll help.

GROUP LEADER: [*Records the second consequence. Requests and diagrams a new solution.*]

CHILD: If you won't help, I'll hit you.

GROUP LEADER: Can anyone think of what might happen if she hits Brittany?

CHILD: Brittany might punch her back.

CHILD 2: Brittany yells at her.

GROUP LEADER: [*Diagrams consequences of the second solution. After several other solutions and their likely consequences are elicited, asks children to choose the best one and explain that choice.*]

Social Growth Program

Module Nine: Social Problem Solving
For Me

1. Write down one social problem situation (e.g., someone trips you in the lunch line).

    - List three alternative responses.
    - Bring this list to the next group session.
    - The group can talk about consequences.

2. Make a list of two social problems you confront between today and the next group session. Plan to tell the group what happened.

Social Growth Program

Module Nine: Social Problem Solving
For My Parents and Teachers

Child's Name _____

Group Leaders' Names _____

Today's Date _____

    Today's session focused on teaching children how they can think things through and use *problem-solving skills* when faced with social or interpersonal conflict. Because conflict with others is inevitable in children's lives, efforts to help them consider how to respond are important. Children can learn to improve their social problem solving skills.

    We began working on the three parts of social problem solving. These are (1) thinking of alternative responses, (2) thinking of the consequences of each response, and (3) choosing the best response.

    As an example, consider this situation: Sally wants Jeffrey to help her build a tower of blocks. Possible solutions and their consequences might be:

- Possible Solution
"Will you help me?"

Consequences: He'll help her. He'll say, "Maybe I'll help." He'll say, "No!"

- Second Solution
"If you won't help, I'll punch you."

Consequences: He'll punch her. He'll yell at her. He'll tell the teacher.

    During our session we considered a number of similar problem situations. For each one the children talked about possible solutions and what their consequences might be. We began working on selecting the best solution and talking about reasons for our choice.

Additional Comments:

INDIVIDUAL SESSION

Preparation Ideas for the Individual Session

Little preparation is required for this module. The therapist may want to refer to "Social Problem Situations" (included in the preparation ideas for the group session) for examples of social problems that can be used to emphasize the frequency of social conflicts and the importance of social problem solving. These examples could be used to supplement those offered by the child. The therapist may also plan to use some of these situations during the section on alternative and consequential thinking, although each child's "real-life" examples sometimes produce livelier discussions.

Guidelines for Conducting the Individual Session

Introduction

The module might be introduced in this way:

We have been practicing many skills that help us get along well with others. The skills of listening, giving positive messages, and empathy will help us to make friends, keep friends, and avoid some conflicts with others. But despite our very best efforts, some conflicts with others are bound to happen. This is because what we want and need, or what we think is right, will not always match what others want or need or think is right.

The therapist should record the conflict situation without questioning or discussing *how* the child handled the conflict. This will diminish fears of evaluation and contribute to the success of the brainstorming activity. The therapist can also contribute ideas to the list, referring to the preparation ideas as needed. After generating the list of situations, the therapist discusses with the child the impossibility of completely avoiding such conflicts and offers the positive message that we can learn how to solve these conflicts in ways that help us maintain friendships.

Developing Alternative Thinking

The therapist presents the task of alternative thinking within the framework of a game:

Let's play a game. The idea of this game is to think of lots of different ways to act or behave when we face conflicts with other people. Let's start with one of the conflicts that we have listed. Which one would you like to start with?

The therapist records the chosen conflict on a new sheet of paper and repeats that the idea is to think of lots of different ways to deal with the problem. The therapist should listen to all possibilities in as accepting and noncritical a way as possible. Sometimes the therapist can note that one suggestion is an elaboration of another and can then offer a totally different alternative. This modeling will help the child to think in more diverse ways.

Developing Consequential Thinking

The therapist might say:

> Now let's think about the consequences or results of each of these solutions. What is a consequence? A consequence is an outcome of something that we do. It might be the reaction of a second person to something we have done or said. For example, if Sam hits Sarah, Sarah might hit Sam back, tell Sam's mother, cry, walk away, or tell Sam that she didn't like that. We don't know exactly what will happen, but we can think about what might happen. Let's begin by choosing one of the problem situations for which we've identified many possible solutions.

It is helpful to choose a problem situation that is conducive to naming consequences. Sometimes a problem situation that involves something concrete like refusal to share is a good way to begin, because solutions such as hit, grab, ask, and tell someone are usually generated.

Finally, the therapist helps the child consider the pros and cons of each solution offered. The therapist takes the role of facilitator during this consideration of consequences; that is, whenever possible, the therapist refrains from listing consequences and encourages the child's input. This evolves into a discussion of "Which solution might be the best one?"

Social Growth Program

Module Nine: Social Problem Solving
For My Parents

Child's Name _____

Leader's Name _____

Today's Date _____

   Today we talked about how we cannot avoid conflicts with our brothers or sisters, friends and classmates, parents and teachers. Some conflicts are bound to occur because what we want or what we think is right will not be the same for everyone. We began to learn how we can think things through and use problem-solving skills when faced with these social conflicts.

   We began learning about the three parts of social problem solving. These are (1) Thinking of alternative responses, (2) Thinking of the consequences of each response, and (3) Choosing the best response. As an example, consider this situation: Sally wants Jeffrey to help her build a tower of blocks. Possible solutions and their consequences might be:

- Possible Solution

   "Will you help me?"

Consequences: He'll help her. He'll say "Maybe I'll help. "He'll say "No!"

- Second Solution

   "If you won't help, I'll punch you."

Consequences: He'll punch her. He'll yell at her. He'll tell the teacher.

   We talked about some of the conflicts that _____ has encountered. Next week we will continue our work on this by talking about alternative solutions and their consequences.

Additional Comments:

BIBLIOGRAPHY

Achenbach, L., & Edelbrock, C. (1983). *Manual for the Child Behavior Checklist and Revised Child Behavior Profile*. Burlington, VT: Department of Psychiatry, University of Vermont.

Amidon, E. J., & Hoffman, C. (1965). Can teachers help the socially rejected? *Elementary School Journal, 66,* 149–154.

Archer, C. (1984). Children's attitudes toward sex-role divisions in adult occupational roles. *Sex Roles, 10,* 1–10.

Asher, S. R., & Renshaw, P. D. (1981). Children without friends: Social knowledge and social skill training. In S. R. Asher & J. M. Gottman (Eds.), *The development of children's friendships*. New York: Cambridge University Press.

Bandura, A. (1977). *Social learning theory*. Englewood Cliffs, NJ: Prentice-Hall.

Bandura, A., & Walters, R. H. (1963). *Social learning and personality development*. New York: Holt, Rinehart and Winston.

Bierman, K. L., Miller, C. L. & Stabb, S. D. (1987). Improving the social behavior and peer acceptance of rejected boys: Effects of social skill training with instructions and prohibitions. *Journal of Consulting and Clinical Psychology, 55,*(2), 194–200.

Bigelow, B. J. (1977). Children's friendship expectations: A cognitive-developmental study. *Child Development, 48,* 246–253.

Bigelow, B. J., & LaGaipa, J. J. (1975). Children's written descriptions of friendship: A multidimensional analysis. *Developmental Psychology, 11,* 857–858.

Bonney, M. E. (1971). Assessment of efforts to aid socially isolated elementary school pupils. *Journal of Educational Research, 64,* 345–364.

Buss, A. H., & Plomin, R. (1975). *A temperament theory of personality development*. New York: Wiley.

Buswell, M. M. (1953). The relationship between social structure of the classroom and the academic successes of the pupils. *Journal of Experimental Education, 22,* 37–52.

Cairns, R. B. (1979). *Social development: The origins and plasticity of interchanges*. San Francisco: Freeman.

Cassidy, J., & Asher, S. R. (1989). Loneliness and peer relations in young children [Abstract]. *Abstracts: Biennial Meeting of the Society for Research in Child Development, 6,* 211.

Chandler, C. L., Weissberg, R. P., Cowen, E. L., and Guare, J. (1984). Long-term effects of a school-based secondary prevention program for young mal-adaptive children. *Journal of Consulting and Clinical Psychology, 52*(2), 165–170.

Combs, T. P, & Slaby, D. A. (1978). Social skills training with children. In B. Lahey & A. Kazdin (Eds.), *Advances in clinical child psychology: Vol. 1*. New York: Plenum Press.

Conley, J. J. (1985). Longitudinal stability of personality traits: A multitrait-multimethod-multioccasion analysis. *Journal of Personality and Social Psychology, 49*, 1266–1282.

Corsaro, W. A. (1981). Friendship in nursery school: Social organization in a peer environment. In S. R. Asher & J. M. Gottman (Eds.), *The development of children's friendships*. New York: Cambridge University Press.

Cowen, E. L., Gesten, E., and Wilson, A. (1979). The Primary Mental Health Project (PMHP): Evaluation of current program effectiveness. *American Journal of Community Psychology, 7*, 293–303.

Cowen, E. L., Pederson, A., Babigian, M., Izzo, L. D., & Trost, M. A. (1973). Long-term folllow-up of early detected vulnerable children. *Journal of Consulting and Clinical Psychology, 41*, 438–446.

Cowen, E. L., Spinell, A., Wright, S., and Weissberg, R. P. (1983). Continuing dissemination of a school-based mental health program. *Professional Psychology, 13*, 118–127.

Cowen, E. L., Trost, M. A., Lorion, R. P., Dorr, D., Izzo, L. D., and Isaacson, R. V. (1975). *New ways in school mental health: Early detection and prevention of school maladaptation*. New York: Human Sciences Press.

Cowen, E. L., Weissberg, R., Lotyczewski, M., Bromley, M., Gilliland-Mallo, R., DeMeis, J., Farago, J., Grassi, R., Haffey, W., Weiner, M., and Woods, A. (1983). Validity generalization of a school-based preventative mental health program. *Professional Psychology: Research and Practice, 14*, 613–623.

Cowen, E. L., Zax, M., Izzo, L. D., and Trost, M. A. (1966). Prevention of emotional disorders in the school setting: A further investigation. *Journal of Counseling and Clinical Psychology, 30*, 381–387.

Damon, W. (1977). *The social world of the child*. San Francisco: Jossey-Bass.

Denham, S., and Almeida, N. C. (1987). Children's social problem-solving skills, behavioral adjustment and interventions: A meta-analysis evaluating theory and practice. *Journal of Applied-Developmental Psychology, 8*(4), 391–409.

Dodge, K. A., McClaskey, C. L., & Feldman, E. (1985). Situational approach to the assessment of social competence in children. *Journal of Consulting and Clinical Psychology, 53*(3), 344–353.

Dohrenwend, B. P., Dohrenwend, B. S., Gould, M. S., Link, B., Neugebauer, R., and Wunschhitzig, R. (1980). *Mental illness in the United States: Epidemiological estimates*. New York: Praeger.

Dohrenwend, B. P., Dohrenwend, B. S., Gould, M. S., Link, B., Neugebauer, R., & Wunschhitzig, R. (1980). *Mental illness in the United States: Epidemiological estimates*. New York: Praeger.

Durlak, J. (1985). Primary prevention of school maladjustment. *Journal of Consulting and Clinical Psychology, 53*(5), 623–630.

Eysenck, H. J. (Ed.). (1981). *A model for personality*. New York: Springer.

Feiring, C. C. (1981, April). The social network of three-year-old children. Paper presented at the Society for Research on Child Development, Boston.

Furman, W. (1987). Acquaintanceship in middle childhood. *Developmental Psychology, 23,* 563–570.

Gesten, E. L. (1976). A health resources inventory: The development of a measure of the personal and social competence of primary-grade children. *Journal of Consulting and Clinical Psychology, 44,* 775–786.

Glidewell, J. C., & Swallow, C. S. (1969). *The prevalence of maladjustment in elementary schools. Report prepared for the Joint Commission on Mental Illness and Health of Children.* Chicago: University of Chicago.

Gottman, J. M. (1983). How children become friends. *Monographs of the Society for Research in Child Development, 48* (3, Serial No. 201).

Gottman, J. M., Gonso, J., & Rasmussen, B. (1975). Social interaction, social competence and friendship in children. *Child Development, 46,* 709–718.

Harter, S. (1983). Developmental perspectives on the self-system. In Paul H. Mussen (Ed.), *Handbook of child psychology: Vol. 4. Socialization, personality, and social development.* New York: Wiley.

Hartup, W. W., Glazer, J. A., & Charlesworth, R. (1967). Peer reinforcement and sociometric status. *Child Development, 38,* 1017–1024.

Hay, D. F. (1979). Cooperative interactions and sharing between very young children and their parents. *Developmental Psychology, 15,* 647–653.

Higgins, E. T. (1981). Role taking and social judgment: Alternative developmental perspectives and processes. In John H. Flavell & Lee Ross (Eds.), *Social cognitive development: Frontiers and possible futures.* Cambridge, England: Cambridge University Press.

Hightower, A. D., & Cowen, E. L. (1984). The Aide-Child Rating Scale. Unpublished manuscript, University of Rochester, Rochester, NY.

Hightower, A. D., Work, W. C., Cowen, E. L., Lotcyzewski, B. S., Spinell, A. P., Guare, J. C., & Rohrbeck, C. A. (1986). The Teacher-Child Rating Scale: A brief objective measure of elementary children's school problem behaviors and competencies. *School Psychology Review, 15*(3), 393–409.

Hopper, R. B., & Kirschenbaum, D. S. (1985). Social problem solving and social competence in preadolescents: Is inconsistency the hobgoblin of little minds? *Cognitive Therapy and Research, 9*(6), 685–701.

Johnson, R. R., Greenspan, S., & Brown, G. M. (1984). Children's ability to recognize and improve upon socially inept communications. *Journal of Genetic Psychology, 144,* 255–264.

Kanfer, F. H., and Karoly, P. (1972). Self-control: A behavioristic excursion into the lion's den. *Behavior Therapy, 3,* 398–416.

Karoly, P., and Kanfer, F. H. (Eds.). (1982). *Self-management and behavior change: From theory to practice.* New York: Pergamon Press.

Kendal, P. C. & Finch, A. J. (1976). A cognitive behavioral treatment for impulsivity: A case study. *Journal of Consulting and Clinical Psychology, 44,* 852–857.

King, C., and Kirschenbaum, D. S. (1990). An experimental evaluation of a school-based program for children at risk: Wisconsin Early Intervention. *Journal of Community Psychology, 18,* 167–177.

Kirschenbaum, D. S.(1979). Social competence intervention and evaluation in the inner city: Cincinnati's Social Skills Developmental Program. *Journal of Consulting and Clinical Psychology, 47,* 778–780.

Kirschenbaum, D. S., Klei, R. G., Brown, J. E. III, and DeVoge, J. B. (1979). A non-experimental, but useful, evaluation of a therapy/consultation early intervention program. In G. Landsberg, W. D. Neigher, R. J. Hammer, C. Windle, and J. R. Woy (Eds.), *Evaluation in Practice: A Sourcebook of Program Evaluation Studies from Mental Health Care Systems in the United States.* Rockville, MD: US Department of Health, Education, and Welfare.

Kirschenbaum, D. S., Bane, S., Fowler, R., Klei, B., Kuykendahl, K., Marsh, M. E., and Pedro, J. L. (1976). *Social Skills Development Program: Handbook for Helping.* Cincinnati: Cincinnati Health Department.

Kirschenbaum, D. S., Pedro-Carroll, J. L., and DeVoge, J. B. (1983). A social competence model meets an early intervention program: Description and evaluation of Cincinnati's Social Skills Development Program. *Origins of Psychopathology: Problems in Research and Public Policy* (pp. 215–250). New York: Cambridge University Press.

Kirschenbaum, D. S. (1983). Toward more behavioral early intervention programs: A rationale. *Professional Psychology: Research and Practice, 14,* 159–169.

Kirschenbaum, D. S., Steffen, J. S. & D'Orta, C. (1978). The social competence classroom behavioral observation system. *Behavioral Analysis and Modification, 2,* 314–322.

Kohlberg, L. (1969). Stage and sequence: The cognitive-developmental approach to socialization. In D. A. Goslin (Ed.), *Handbook of socialization theory and research.* Chicago: Rand McNally.

Ladd, G. (1981). Effectiveness of social learning method for enhancing children's social interaction and peer acceptance. *Child Development, 52,* 171–178.

Ladd, G. W., & Mize, J. (1983). A cognitive-social learning model of social-skill training. *Psychological Review, 90,* 127–157.

Lorion, R. P., Caldwell, R. A., and Cowen, E. L. (1976). Effects of a school mental health project: A one year follow-up. *Journal of School Psychology, 14,* 56–63.

Lorion, R. P., Cowen, E. L., & Caldwell, R. A. (1975). Normative and parametric analyses of school maladjustment. *American Journal of Community Psychology, 3,* 293–301.

Marshall, H. R.. & McCandless, B. R. (1957). Relationships between dependence on adults and social acceptance by peers. *Child Development, 28,* 413–419.

Matson, J. L., Rotatori, A. F., & Helsel, W. J. (1983). Development of a rating scale to measure social skills in children: The Matson Evaluation of Social Skills with Youngsters (MESSY). *Behaviour Research & Therapy, 21*(4), 335–340.

McDavid, J. W., & Harari, H. (1966). Stereotyping of names and popularity in grade school children. *Child Development, 37,* 453–459.

McFall, R. M. (1976). Behavioral training: A skill-acquisition approach to clinical problems. In J. R. Spence, R. C. Carson and J. W. Thibaut (Eds.), *Behavioral approaches to therapy.* Morristown, NJ: General Learning Press.

McKim, B. J., Weissberg, R. P., Cowen, E. L., Gesten, E. L., & Rapkin, D. (1982). A comparison of the problem-solving ability and adjustment of suburban and urban third-grade children. *American Journal of Community Psychology, 10*(2), 155–169.

Meichenbaum, D., & Goodman, J. (1971). Training impulsive children to talk to themselves: A means of developing self-control. *Journal of Abnormal Psychology, 77,* 115–126.

Michelson, L., & Wood, R. (1980). Social skills assessment and training with children and adolescents. In M. Hersen, R. M. Eisler, & P. Miller (Eds.), *Progress in behavior modification: Vol. 9.* New York: Academic Press, 1980.

Michelson, L., Mannarino, A. P., Marchione, K., Stern, M., Figueroa, J. & Beck, S. (1983). A comparative outcome study of behavioral social skills training, interpersonal problem solving, and non-directive control treatments with child psychiatric outpatients: Process, outcome, and generalization effects. *Behavior Research and Therapy, 21,* 545–556.

Michelson, L., Sugai, D. P., Wood, R. P., & Kazdin, A. E. (1983). *Social skills assessment and training with children: An empirically-based handbook.* New York: Plenum Press.

Mischel, W. (1973). Toward a cognitive social learning reconceptualization of personality. *Psychological Review, 80,* 252–283.

Mischel, W. (1986). *Introduction to personality* (4th ed.). New York: Holt, Rinehart & Winston.

Nelson, G., & Carson, P. (1988). Evaluation of a social problem-solving skills program for third- and fourth-grade students. *American Journal of Community Psychology, 16,* 79–99.

Nuttall, E.V., & Ivey, A.E. (1986). The Diagnostic Interview Process. In H. M. Knoff (Ed.), *The assessment of child and adolescent personality.* New York: Guilford Press.

Oden, S. L., and Asher, S. R., (1977). Coaching low accepted children in social skills: A follow-up sociometric assessment. *Child Development, 48,* 496–506.

Pellegrini, D. S. & Urbain, E. S. (1985). An evaluation of interpersonal cognitive problem-solving training with children. *Journal of Child Psychology and Psychiatry, 26*(1), 17–41.

Piaget, J. (1970). Piaget's theory. In P. H. Mussen (Ed.), *Carmichael's manual of child psychology: Vol. 1.* New York: Wiley.

Piaget, J., & Inhelder, B. (1969). *The psychology of the child.* New York: Basic Books.

Powers, S. & Wagner, M. J. (1984). Attributions for school achievement in middle school students. *Journal of Early Adolescence, 4,* 215–222.

Poznanski, E. O., Grossman, J. A., Buchsbaum, Y., Baregas, M., Freeman, L., & Gibbons, R. (1984). Preliminary studies of the reliability and validity of the Children's Depression Rating Scale. *Journal of the American Academy of Child Psychiatry, 23,* 191–197.

Protective Behaviors (1984). *Safe, adventurous, and loving.* Madison, WI: Protective Behaviors, Inc.

Puttalaz, M., & Gottman, J. M. (1981). Social skills and group acceptance. In S. R. Asher & John M. Gottman (Eds.), *The development of children's friendships* (pp. 116–149). New York: Cambridge University Press.

Renshaw, P. D., & Asher, S. R. (1982). Social competence and peer status: A distinction between goals and strategies. In K. H. Rubin and H. S. Ross (Eds.), *Peer relationships and social skills in childhood.* New York: Springer-Verlag.

Richard, B. A., & Dodge, K. A. (1982). School maladjustment and problem-solving in school-aged children. *Journal of Consulting and Clinical Psychology, 50,* 226–233.

Roff, M. (1961). Childhood social interactions and young adult bad conduct. *Journal of Abnormal and Social Psychology, 63,* 333–337.

Roff, M., Sells, S. B., & Golden, M. M. (1972). *Social adjustment and personality development in children.* Minneapolis: University of Minnesota Press.

Rogosch, F. A., & Newcombe, A. F. (1989). Children's perceptions of peer reputations and their social reputations among peers. *Child Development, 60,* 597–610.

Sandler, I. N. (1972). Characteristics of women working as child-aides in a school-based preventive mental health program. *Journal of Consulting and Clinical Psychology, 39,* 56–61.

Savin-Williams, R. C., & Demo, D. H. (1984). Developmental change and stability in adolescent self-concept. *Developmental Psychology, 20,* 1100–1110.

Schaffer, H. R. (1971). Cognitive structure and early social behavior. In H. R. Schaffer (Ed.), *The origins of human social relations.* New York: Academic Press.

Scott, R., Himadi, W., & Keane, T. (1983). A review of generalization in social skills training: Suggestions for further research. In M. Hensen, R. Eiseler, & P. Miller (Eds.), *Progress in behavior modification: Vol. 15.* New York: Academic Press.

Selman, R. L. (1976). Toward a structural analysis of developing interpersonal relationship concepts: Research with normal and disturbed preadolescent boys. In A. Pick (Ed.), *Minnesota Symposia on Child Psychology: Vol. 10.* Minneapolis: University of Minnesota Press.

Shantz, C. U. (1982). Children's understanding of social rules and the social context. In F. C. Serafica (Ed.), *Social-cognitive development in context.* New York: Guilford Press.

Sharp, K. C. (1981). Impact of interpersonal problem-solving training on preschoolers' social competence. *Journal of Applied Developmental Psychology, 2,* 129–143.

Shure, M. B. (1981). Social competence as a problem-solving skill. In J. D. Wine & M. D. Smye (Eds.), *Social Competence* (pp. 158–185). New York: Guilford Press.

Shure, M. B., & Spivack, G. (1972). Means-ends thinking, adjustment, and social class among elementary school-aged children. *Journal of Consulting and Clinical Psychology, 38,* 348–353.

Shure, M. B., & Spivack, G. (1982). Interpersonal problem-solving in young children: A cognitive approach to prevention. *American Journal of Community Psychology, 10*(3), 341–356.

Singleton, L. C., & Asher, S. R. (1977). Peer preferences and social interaction among third-grade children in an integrated school district. *Journal of Educational Psychology, 69,* 330–336.

Spivack, G., Platt, J. J., & Shure, M. B. (1976). *The problem solving approach to adjustment.* San Francisco: Jossey-Bass.

Spivack, G. & Shure, M. B. (1974). *Social adjustment of young children.* San Francisco: Jossey-Bass.

Stein, D. M., & Polyson, J. (1984). The Primary Mental Health Project Reconsidered. *Journal of Consulting and Clinical Psychology, 52,* 940–45.

Stipek, D. J. (1984). Sex differences in children's attributions of success and failure on math and spelling tests. *Sex Roles, 11,* 969–981.

Stoddart, T., & Turiel, E. (1985). Children's concepts of cross-gender activities. *Child Development, 56,* 1241–1252.

Strain, P. S., Cooke, T. P., & Appolloni, T. (1976). *Teaching exceptional children.* New York: Academic Press.

Thomas, A. & Chess, S. (1977). *Temperament and development.* New York: Brunner/Mazel.

Ullmann, C. A. (1957). Teachers, peers, and tests as predictors of adjustment. *Journal of Educational Psychology, 48,* 257–267.

Urbain, E. S. (1980). Interpersonal problem-solving training and social perspective-taking with impulsive children via modeling, role play, and self-instruction. Unpublished doctoral dissertation, University of Minnesota.

Watson, M. W. (1984). Development of social role understanding. *Developmental Review, 4,* 192–213.

Weissberg, R. P., Gesten, E. L., Carnrike, C. L., Toro, P. A., Rapkin, B. D., Davidson, E. & Cowen, E. L. (1981). Social problem-solving skills training: A competence-building intervention with 2nd–4th-grade children. *American Journal of Community Psychology, 9,* 411–424.

Weissburg, R. P., Cowen, E. L., Lotyczewski, B. S., & Gesten, E. L. (1983). The Primary Mental Health Project: Seven consecutive years of outcome research. *Journal of Consulting and Clinical Psychology, 51,* 100–107.

Yarrow, M. R., & Campbell, J. D. (1963). Person perception in children. *Merrill-Palmer Quarterly, 9,* 57–72.

Young, L. L., & Cooper, D. H. (1944). Some factors associated with popularity. *The Journal of Educational Psychology, 35,* 513–535.

Youniss, J., & Volpe, J. A. (1978). A relational analysis of children's friendships. In W. Damon (Ed.), *New directions for child development: Social cognition.* San Francisco: Jossey-Bass.

INDEX

Academic achievement, 50
Acceptance
  of child's thoughts, 83
  peer group, 13
Active listening, 3, 33, 104–13
Adjustment
  impact of training on, 29
  nature and significance of social,
    4–5
  social of young children, 2
Adults, network of trusted, 149,
  154
Aggressive behaviors, 70
Aide-Child Rating Scale, 77, 79
Alternative thinking, 167, 169–70,
  175–76
AML School Adjustment Rating Scale,
  54, 74
Anxieties, social, 56
Asher, S. R., 4, 23
Asking questions, 3, 33, 123–32
Assessment, 73
  individual, 55–67
  of social adjustment problems, 51
Assessment data, 70
  integrating, 72
Assessment instruments, 3, 77
Attempting to learn a new skill, 158

Behavior
  ability to change one's, 156
  acquisition and maintenance of
    socially skilled, 10–12
  managing, 159
  personal determinants of, 17
Behavioral interview, 56–57

Behavioral rating scales, 57–58
Behavioral skills, deficit in, 56
Behaviors
  aggressive, 70
  changing social, 14–16
  desirable, 11
  in multiple settings, 61
Belonging, 93
Bierman, K. L., 25
Brainstorming, 85, 96, 120, 124, 149,
  154

Case illustration, 70–73
Cassidy, J., 4
Causal thinking, 167, 171–72
Chandler, C. L., 22
Chart, 134
Child, uniqueness of every, 6
Child Behavior Checklist, 77, 79
Child-focused programs, 20
Children
  identifying at risk, 51
  modeling
    active listening between, 107–08
    among, 98
    asking questions between, 127
    sharing feelings between, 137
    standing up for me, 146, 148
    warm messages between, 116
  popular, 4
  targeted for services, 35
  unpopular, 4
Children's Assertive Behavior Scale,
  58
Children's Depression Rating Scale-
  Revised, 77, 78